Nick Vandome

Android Tablets
for Seniors

in easy steps

3rd Edition

Covers Android 7.0 Nougat

In easy steps is an imprint of In Easy Steps Limited
16 Hamilton Terrace · Holly Walk · Leamington Spa
Warwickshire · United Kingdom · CV32 4LY
www.ineasysteps.com

Notice of Liability
Every effort has been made to ensure that this book contains accurate
and current information. However, In Easy Steps Limited and the
author shall not be liable for any loss or damage suffered by readers
as a result of any information contained herein.

Trademarks
All trademarks are acknowledged as belonging to their respective
companies.

In Easy Steps Limited supports The Forest Stewardship Council (FSC),
the leading international forest certification organisation. All our titles
that are printed on Greenpeace approved FSC certified paper carry the
FSC logo.

MIX
Paper from
responsible sources
FSC® C020837

Printed and bound in the United Kingdom

ISBN 978-1-84078-766-5

Contents

1 Introducing Android Tablets   7

About Tablets	8
About Android	12
Tablet Terms Explained	14
Using a Touchscreen	16
Using Apps	18
Makes and Models	20
Android and Google	22
Creating a Google Account	24
Turning On and Controls	26
Setting Up Your Tablet	27
Adding Accessories	28

2 Getting Started with Your Tablet   29

Viewing the Home Screen	30
Navigating Around	31
Adding Apps	32
Moving Apps	33
Working with Favorites	34
Adding Widgets	35
Changing the Background	36
Creating Folders	37
Using Notifications	38
Screen Rotation	40
Accessing Settings	41
Quick Settings	44
Editing Quick Settings	45
Locking Your Tablet	46
Searching	48
Ok Google	51
Using Google Feeds	52

3   At Your Fingertips   57

The Android Keyboard   58
Keyboard Settings   60
Keyboard Shortcuts   62
Adding Text   64
Working with Text   65
Creating a Dictionary   66

4   Working with Apps   67

About Android Apps   68
Built-in Apps   69
Multitasking with Apps   72
Around the Play Store   74
Finding Apps   76
Downloading Apps   78
Deleting Apps   80
Updating Apps   81
App Information   82

5   Useful Apps   83

Staying Organized   84
Being Productive   86
Keeping Entertained   88
Lifestyle   90
Health and Fitness   94
Family History   98

6   Tablet Entertainment   99

Using Google Play   100
Music on Android   101
Downloading Music   102

Playing Music 104
Managing Music 107
Pinning Music 108
Movies and TV Shows 110
Obtaining Books 114
Around an Ebook 116
Adding Notes 118
Adding Bookmarks 120
Definitions and Translations 121
Using Cameras 122
Adding Photos 124
Viewing Photos 126
Adding Folders 129
Editing Photos 130
Sharing Photos 132

7 Keeping in Touch 133

Email on Android 134
Adding Email Accounts 135
Using Email 137
Email Settings 139
Social Networking 140
Keeping an Address Book 142
Using Your Calendar 144
Using Your Google Account 146

8 Browsing the Web 147

Android Web Browsers 148
Opening Pages 149
Bookmarking Pages 150
Links and Images 152
Using Tabs 153
Being Incognito 154
Browser Settings 155

9 On Your Travels 157

Traveling with Your Tablet	158
Keeping Your Tablet Safe	160
Airport Security	161
Finding Hotels and Flights	162
Calling with Skype	164
Useful Travel Apps	166

10 Sharing with the Family 169

About Multiple Users	170
Adding Family Members	172
Switching Between Users	174
Guest Users	175
Restricted Profiles	176

11 Accessibility and Security 177

Accessibility	178
Security Issues	180
About Antivirus Apps	181
Using Antivirus Apps	182
Locating Your Tablet	184

Index 187

1 Introducing Android Tablets

Tablet computers and the Android operating system are an ideal match for anyone who wants their computing as mobile and as flexible as possible. This chapter introduces the basics of Android tablets and setting them up.

8   About Tablets

12 About Android

14 Tablet Terms Explained

16 Using a Touchscreen

18 Using Apps

20 Makes and Models

22 Android and Google

24 Creating a Google Account

26 Turning On and Controls

27 Setting Up Your Tablet

28 Adding Accessories

About Tablets

Tablet computers are the result of the desire for our computing devices to become smaller and more portable (from desktops, to laptops, to tablets), and the evolution of mobile operating systems, initially introduced for smartphones. The combination of the two has resulted in the birth and increasing popularity of tablets; they are small, portable for almost any situation, and customizable. They are also powerful enough to perform most everyday computing functions, such as email, using the web, word processing and communicating with social networking sites.

Android is now owned by Google.

The New icon pictured above indicates a new or enhanced feature introduced with the latest version of Android 7.0 Nougat for tablets.

Tablets are essentially small computers that run on a mobile operating system, rather than those used on desktop and laptop computers, such as Windows and macOS. They can be used as an addition to your suite of computing products or they could even be considered as a replacement for items such as desktop computers or laptops, depending on your computing needs. But for most types of mobile computing tasks, tablets are definitely the established choice on the digital block.

Android operating system

All computers need an operating system to make them work and perform all of the required tasks for the user. For tablets, the two main operating systems are iOS for Apple tablets (the iPad, iPad Pro and iPad Mini) and Android. The latter has been developed through its use on smartphones and is now a significant player in the tablet market. The fact that it is issued on both types of device means that if you have an Android smartphone then an Android tablet is a perfect match.

Android is an open source operating system, which means that developers and manufacturers can work with the source code to tailor it to their own needs and devices (as long as they meet certain requirements and standards). Android tablets are made by a number of different manufacturers and although the hardware differs between devices, the Android operating system is common between them (although the versions of Android differs between devices; see page 13). Android tablets generally come in 7-inch to 10-inch models.

It is now "apps" instead of "programs"

The functionality of tablets can be expanded almost endlessly through the inclusion of apps: computer programs that either come pre-installed or can be downloaded from a linked service. For Android tablets, this service is provided by the Google Play Store, which is accessed via an app on the tablet or via the Google Play website on a computer. You will need a Google Account to buy or get items from the Google Play Store (see pages 24-25 for details about creating an account). Some models of tablet also have their own proprietary online store for buying apps, but they will also have the Play Store, which generally will have a larger range of apps available.

Apps are denoted by the thumbnail icons that appear on the tablet's Home screen (and also in the All Apps area).

Microsoft Windows can also be used on tablets, and Microsoft has its own tablet, Surface, which uses Windows.

For more information about specific makes and models of Android tablets see pages 20-21.

...cont'd

Touchscreen

Tablets are touchscreen devices, which means that their functionality and controls are accessed by tapping, swiping or pressing on the screen. This includes the keyboard, which appears automatically on the screen if data input is required, e.g. for writing an email, entering a website address or filling in an online form. For people who have always used a physical keyboard, the virtual one can take a bit of getting used to, particularly if you are doing a lot of typing, but the more you use it, the more familiar it will become.

✓ My shopping list											
Editing									07/04/2015 15:06

Pasta
Steak
Orange juice
Cereal |

: ; " ( ) 🎤

q	w	e	r	t	y	u	i	o	p	⌫
a	s	d	f	g	h	j	k	l	↵
⬆	z	x	c	v	b	n	m	!	?	⬆
?123	,						.	🙂

Getting connected to the internet

One of the essential functions of tablets is internet connectivity, for accessing the web and also the range of Android services that are connected to Google apps and online services.

The standard form of online connectivity for tablets is provided by Wi-Fi. This will connect to the internet via your own Wi-Fi router and service provider in your home, or through a Wi-Fi hotspot if you are traveling with your tablet. Some models of tablets also have 3G/4G connectivity. This is wireless, mobile access to the internet, provided by telecoms companies through either a monthly plan or pay-as-you-go options. This provides access to the internet without the need for Wi-Fi.

Don't forget

If your tablet has 3G/4G connectivity, you will have to pay for this service from an appropriate provider, in the same way as obtaining internet access for a smartphone. Only some models of tablet have this type of connectivity.

Hybrid tablets

In computing terms, the current tablet market is a relatively new one and manufacturers are developing ideas in terms of the evolution of the tablet, particularly in relation to the more traditional laptop. Nothing stays the same forever and this is exaggerated in the computing world where change can be particularly fast. Just as the laptop has taken over from the desktop as the main computing device for the majority of people, the tablet is beginning to make people think about the next stage in the evolution of personal computing and how we interact with the digital world.

Some manufacturers have developed hybrid tablets that are designed to bridge the gap between tablets and laptops. These devices can be used as self-contained tablets, using the virtual touchscreen keyboard, or they can be docked to a physical keyboard and be used more like a laptop.

The removable keyboards that come with hybrid tablets are not as sturdy as those on a traditional laptop and their size is usually restricted to the width of the tablet.

As the tablet market develops and evolves further it is likely that there will be more hybrid models, and in time, tablets could begin to replace laptops for a lot of our mobile computing needs.

About Android

Android is essentially a mobile computing operating system, i.e. for mobile devices such as smartphones and tablets.

Android is an open source operating system, which means that the source code is made available to hardware manufacturers and developers so that they can design their devices and apps in conjunction with Android. This has created a large community of Android developers, and also means that Android is not tied to one specific device; individual manufacturers can use it (as long as they meet certain specific criteria), which leads to Android being available on a variety of different devices.

Android Inc was founded in 2003 and the eponymous operating system was initially developed for smartphones. Google quickly saw this as an opportunity to enter the cell phone and computing market, and bought Android in 2005. The first Android-powered smartphone appeared in 2008 and since then has gone from strength to strength. Android-based smartphones make up a majority of the worldwide market, and tablets running Android also enjoy a similar success in terms of market share.

The main differences between the Android operating system and desktop- or laptop-based ones such as Windows or macOS are:

- **No file structure**. There is no built-in File Explorer or Finder structure for storing and managing files. All content is saved within the app in which it is created.

- **Self-contained apps**. Because there is no file structure, apps are generally self-contained and do not communicate with each other.

- **Numerous Home screens**. Rather than just one Desktop, there are numerous Home screens on an Android tablet and they can be used to store and access apps.

- **Content is saved automatically as it is created**.

Don't forget

Android is based on the flexible and robust Linux operating system and shares many similarities with it.

Updating Android

Since Android is open source and can be used on a variety of different devices, this can sometimes cause delays in updating the operating system on the full range of Android devices. This is because it has to be tailored specifically for each different device; it is not a case of 'one size fits all'. This can lead to delays in the latest version being rolled-out to all compatible devices. The product cycle for new versions is usually six to nine months.

Since Android is a Google product, their own devices are usually the first ones to run the latest version of the software. Therefore, the Google Pixel C and Nexus range are the first tablets with Android, 7.0 Nougat, while others are still running previous versions such as 4.3 Jelly Bean, 4.4 KitKat, 5.0 Lollipop or 6.0 Marshmallow. For recently-released tablets, an upgrade to the latest version of Android will be scheduled into the update calendar. However, for some older Android tablets and smartphones, the latest version of the software is not always made available. This can be because of hardware limitations but there have also been suggestions that it is a move by hardware manufacturers, designed to ensure that consumers upgrade to the latest products.

The version of the Android operating system that is being used on your tablet can be viewed from within the **System** > **About tablet** (**Tablet status**) section of the **Settings** app. This is where the operating system can also be updated when a new version is available.

Updated versions of Android are named alphabetically after items of confectionery.

The latest version of Android is 7.0 Nougat. This is available on Google's Pixel and Nexus range of tablets. However, other Android tablets will have a range of earlier versions of Android, which may or may not be upgradable to Nougat. This book covers Android 7.0 Nougat on a Google tablet, but much of the functionality is the same as for earlier versions of Android.

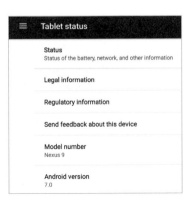

All tablets run on internal batteries which usually offer up to approximately 10 hours of average usage. Tablet batteries can be charged with a USB adapter that connects via the tablet's micro USB port with a supplied cable. This can also be connected to a desktop or laptop computer, but this takes longer to charge the tablet than using the dedicated adapter.

To save battery consumption, turn down the screen brightness (**Settings > Display > Brightness level**) and turn off Wi-Fi and Bluetooth if not in use (**Settings > Wi-Fi/ Bluetooth**).

Tablet Terms Explained

As with any computing device, there is a significant amount of jargon that can be used in relation to tablets. Much of this is similar to that used for desktop and laptop computers, while some is more specific to tablets themselves.

● **Processor**. Also known as the central processing unit, or CPU, this refers to the processing of digital data as it is provided by apps (programs) on the tablet. The more powerful the processor, the quicker the data is interpreted.

● **Memory**. This closely relates to the processor and is also known as random-access memory, or RAM. This type of memory manages the apps that are being run and the commands that are being executed. The greater the amount of memory there is, the quicker the apps will run. With more RAM they will also be more stable and less likely to crash. In the current range of tablets, memory is measured in megabytes (MB) or gigabytes (GB).

● **Storage**. This refers to the amount of digital information that the tablet can store. In the current range of tablets, storage is measured in gigabytes. There are no external signs of processor or memory on a tablet but the details are available from within the **Device** > **Storage** section of the **Settings** app.

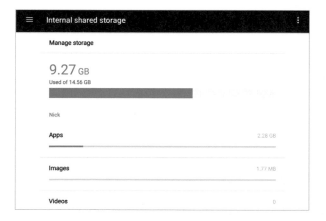

- **Operating System (OS).** This is what links together the hardware and software of the tablet and gives it its functionality. Android is the operating system that is used on a range of different models of tablets, and is widely used throughout the world.

- **Connectivity.** This refers to how the tablet connects to the internet. This is either by Wi-Fi via a compatible router or through mobile access using 3G or 4G, which requires the use of an appropriate, paid-for service.

- **Graphics card.** This is a device that enables images, video and animations to be displayed on the tablet. It is also sometimes known as a video card. The faster the graphics card, the better the quality the relevant media will be displayed at.

- **Wireless.** This refers to a tablet's ability to connect wirelessly to a network, usually via Wi-Fi.

- **Ports.** These are the parts of a tablet into which items can be plugged, such as the micro USB cable for charging the tablet or connecting it to a computer, an HDMI port for connecting the tablet to a high definition TV, and the headphone jack.

- **Camera.** Most tablets have one or two built-in cameras that can be used to take photographs and videos, or communicate via video with other people. There is usually a front-facing camera on most tablets, for video calls, and some also have a rear-facing one for taking higher quality photos and videos.

- **Sensors.** These include a gyroscope for auto-rotating the tablet when it is moved from landscape to portrait, and a GPS sensor.

- **Apps.** These are the programs on the tablet. See pages 18-19 for more details.

- **Touchscreen.** See pages 16-17 for details.

Android Nougat supports high-performance 3D graphics, making it ideal for watching movies or playing games.

Wi-Fi is the most common way to connect wirelessly to the internet on tablets. This is done by connecting with a wireless network access point, such as a public wireless hotspot, or your own home router.

Using a Touchscreen

The traditional method of interacting with a computer is by using a mouse and a keyboard as the input devices. However, this has all changed with tablets; they are much more tactile devices that are controlled by tapping and swiping on the touchscreen. This activates and controls the apps and settings on the tablet, and enables you to add content with the virtual keyboard that appears at the appropriate times.

Gently does it

Touchscreens are sensitive devices and only require a light touch to activate the required command. To get the best out of your touchscreen:

If you are using your tablet in an area where there is likely to be moisture, such as in the kitchen if you are following a recipe, cover the touchscreen in some form of light plastic wrap to protect it from any spills or splashes.

- Tap, swipe or press gently on the screen. Do not use excessive force and do not keep tapping with increasing pressure if something does not work in the way in which you expected. Instead, try performing another action and then returning to the original one.

- Tap with your fingertip rather than your fingernail. This will be more effective in terms of performing the required operation and better for the surface of the touchscreen.

- For the majority of touchscreen tasks, tap, press or swipe at one point on the screen. The exception to this is zooming in and out on certain items (such as web pages), which can be done by pinching inwards and outwards with thumb and forefinger.

- Keep your touchscreen dry and make sure that your fingers are also clean and free of moisture.

- Use a cover to protect the screen when not in use, particularly if you are carrying your tablet in a jacket pocket or a bag.

- Use a screen cloth to keep the screen clean and free of fingerprints and smears. The touchscreen should still work if it has fingerprints and marks on it, but it will become harder to see clearly what is on the screen.

Touchscreen controls

Touchscreens can be controlled with three main types of action. These are:

- **Tapping**. Tap once on an item, such as an app, to activate it. This can also be used for the main navigation control buttons at the bottom of the touchscreen, or for items such as checkboxes when applying settings for specific items.

- **Pressing**. Press and hold on an item on the Home screen to move its position or place it in the **Favorites Tray** at the bottom of the screen. This action can also be used to select text, and access cut, copy and paste options.

- **Swiping**. Swipe down from the top of the Home screen to access the **Notifications Area** and the **Quick Settings**, and swipe up from the bottom of the screen to access the **Google Search** box.

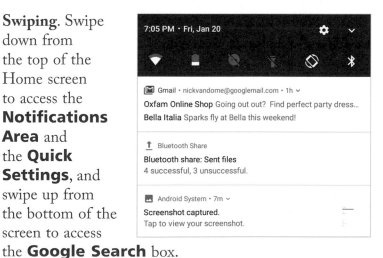

Don't forget

For more information about working with apps on the Home screen, the Notifications Area and the Quick Settings, see Chapter Two.

17

Using Apps

One of the great selling points for Android tablets is the range of apps available from third-party developers. Because Android is open source it is relatively easy for these developers to write apps for Android devices. At the time of writing there are approximately 2.6 million Android apps on the market. Some are free, while others have to be paid for.

The built-in apps are the ones that give the initial functionality to your tablet and include items such as email, a web browser, calendar, calculator and maps. They appear as icons on your tablet's Home screen, or in the All Apps area, and are accessed by tapping lightly on them once.

Don't forget

If your tablet is running low on memory it will automatically close any open apps, to free up more memory. The ones that have been inactive for the longest period of time are the ones that are closed first, until enough memory has been freed up.

Don't forget

Swipe up and down in the All Apps window to view all of the apps on the tablet.

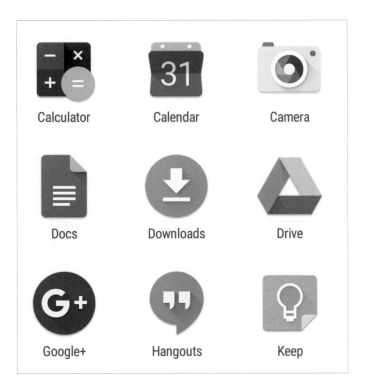

Calculator	Calendar	Camera
Docs	Downloads	Drive
Google+	Hangouts	Keep

New apps for Android tablets are available through the Play Store, or directly from the developer's website. They can be downloaded from there and will then appear on your tablet.

Play Store

Managing apps

Unless otherwise specified, Android apps are self-contained and do not interact with each other on your tablet. This reduces the risk of viruses spreading through your tablet and also contributes to its memory management.

When you switch from one app to another you do not have to close down the original one that you were using. Android keeps it running in the background, but in a state of hibernation so that it is not using up any memory or processing power on your tablet. To do this:

For more information about the Navigation controls (including the Home button and Back button) see page 31.

1 Tap on an app to open it and move through its screens as required

Calendar

2 Tap on the **Home** button on the tablet's Navigation bar at the bottom of the screen to return to the Home screen at any point. The app will remain open in the background

3 Tap on another app to open it while the original app remains open in the background

Play Store

You can also move back to the Home screen by tapping on the **Back** button. This takes you back through the screens that you have accessed within the app, until you reach the app's Home screen, at which point the next screen back will be the tablet's Home screen. If you do this, the next time you access the app it will open at its own Home screen.

Makes and Models

Due to the open source nature of Android it can be used on a range of different devices, and several manufacturers use it on their tablets. Two of the main Android tablet manufacturers are Google and Samsung, who both produce a range of tablets in terms of size and power.

Google Pixel C and Nexus

Until September 2015, Google's flagship tablet was the Nexus 9, running the very latest version of Android (now Android 7.0 Nougat). This was superseded by the Pixel C, a 10-inch tablet that also runs the latest version of Android. The specifications for the Pixel C are higher than the Nexus, but they both have similar functionality in terms of the Android operating system.

Pixel C/Nexus controls

As with most tablets, there are also various touchscreen controls that are located at the bottom of the screen:

1 Frequently-used apps can be pinned in the Favorites Tray at the bottom of the screen, above the Navigation buttons

2 Use this button to view All Apps

3 The dots above the All Apps button indicate how many Home screens are available. Tap on a dot to move to that Home screen (or swipe between them)

Don't forget

Most tablets have versions that can connect to mobile data networks, in the same way as a smartphone, using 3G or 4G services. These have to be paid for through the appropriate service provider, and will then provide mobile internet access even when you do not have Wi-Fi access.

Don't forget

On some models of tablet, the All Apps button is located in the top right-hand corner of the screen.

Samsung tablets

Samsung have a long history of using Android on their tablets, and they have a wide range of these on the market. Some run on earlier versions of Android and it is not always possible to upgrade them to more up-to-date versions for the operating system. The flagship Samsung tablets are (at the time of printing) the Galaxy Tab A and E and the Galaxy Tab S2, all of which should either come with Android Nougat, or be upgradable to it.

Samsung controls

The controls on Samsung tablets are similar to the Pixel C/Nexus, except that they are on the body of the device rather than on the touchscreen, and they are, from left to right: the Recently-used app button, the Home screen button and the Back button.

Don't forget

Samsung tablets have their own range of apps, in addition to the ones available from the Google Play Store. The Play Store apps for functions such as playing music and videos, and reading books and magazines, can be downloaded if they are not pre-installed on a Samsung tablet.

Asus

The latest Asus Android tablet is the ZenPad, although the range may not be upgradable to Android Nougat.

Lenovo

This includes the Yoga range of tablets that have high quality 10-inch screens and are excellent options for viewing TV, and have other multimedia

functionality including, with one model, a built-in projector.

Sony Xperia

This includes a range of 8-inch and 10-inch tablets that have high specifications, which are particularly good for gaming.

Android and Google

Most tablets are linked to a specific company for the provision of their services and selection of apps: Apple for the iPad, Amazon for the Kindle Fire and Google for tablets using Android. As with the other tablets, for Android tablets you must have a linked account to get the most out of your tablet. This is a Google Account, and is created free of charge with a Google email address (Gmail) and a password. Once it has been created, your Google Account will give you access to a number of the built-in Android apps, and also additional services such as backing up and storing your content.

When you first set up your tablet, you can enter your Google Account details or select to create a new account. You can also do this at any time by accessing one of the apps that requires access to a Google Account. These include:

- **Play Store**, for obtaining more apps.

- **Play Movies & TV**.

- **Play Books**.

- **Play Newsstand**.

- **Contacts**, for your online address book. When you enter contact details, these are made available from any web-enabled device.

If you already have a Gmail Account, this will also serve as your Google Account and the login details (email address and password) can be used for both.

When you buy anything through your Google Account, such as music, apps or movies, you will have to enter your credit or debit card details and these will be used for future purchases through your Google Account.

When you access one of these apps you will be prompted to create a Google Account if you have not already linked an existing account. You do not have to do so at this point, but it will give you access to the full range of Google Account services.

Add your account

Google

Sign in to get the most out of your device. Learn more

Email or phone

Or create a new account

NEXT >

Other apps, such as the Photos app for storing and viewing photos, can be used on their own, but if a Google Account has been set up, the content will be backed up automatically.

Some of the benefits of a Google Account include:

- Access from any computer or mobile device with web access, from the page **accounts.google.com** Once you have entered your account details you can access the online Google services, including your Calendar, Gmail and the Play Store.

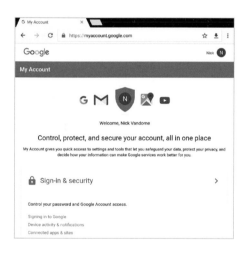
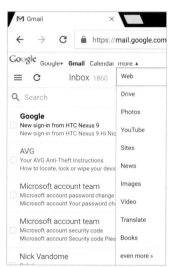

If you buy items from the Play Store through your Google Account on the web, they will also be available on your Android tablet.

- Keep your content synchronized and backed up. With a Google Account, all of your linked data will be automatically synchronized so that it is available for all web-enabled devices, and it will also be backed up by the Google servers.

- Peace of mind that your content is protected. There is a **Security** section on your Google Account web page where you can apply various security settings and alerts.

A new Google Account can also be created within **Settings > Accounts** on your tablet. Tap on the **Add account** button and then tap on the **Google** button. Then enter the required details for the new Google Account (see pages 24-25).

Creating a Google Account

A new Google Account can be created in the following different ways:

- During the initial setup of your Android tablet.

- When you first access one of the relevant apps, as shown on page 22.

- From the **Settings** app and selecting the **Accounts > Add an account** option.

For each of the above, the process for creating the Google Account is the same:

Hot tip

During the account setup process there is also a screen for account recovery, where you can add an answer to a question so that your account details can be retrieved by Google if you forget them.

1 On the **Add your account** screen, tap on the **Or create a new account** button

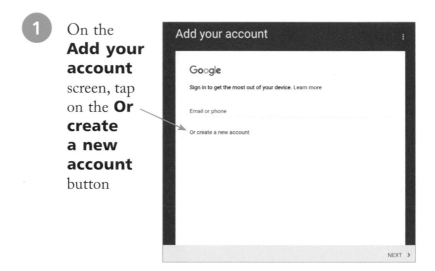

2 Enter your first and last name for the new account and tap on the **Next** button

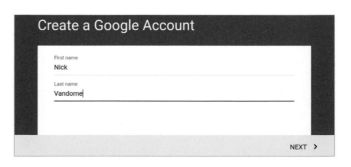

3 Enter a username (this will also become your Gmail address) and tap on the **Next** button at the bottom of the screen

How you'll sign in

You'll use this username to sign in to your Google Account

Username
nickvan729   @gmail.com

Only use A-Z, a-z, and 0-9

Suggested usernames:

NEXT >

Beware

If your chosen username has already been taken, you will be prompted to amend it. This can usually be done by adding a sequence of numbers to the end of it, but make sure you remember the sequence correctly.

4 Create a password for the account and then re-enter it for confirmation. Tap on the **Next** button at the bottom of the screen

Create password

Create a strong password with a mix of letters, numbers and symbols

Create password
••••••••

At least 8 characters   Strong

Confirm password
••••••••

NEXT >

5 Enter your email address and password, and tap on the **Next** button (further down the screen) to sign in with your new account

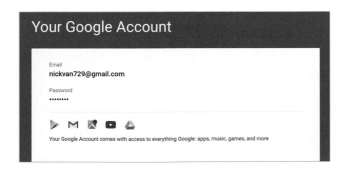

Your Google Account

Email
nickvan729@gmail.com

Password
••••••••

Your Google Account comes with access to everything Google: apps, music, games, and more

Turning On and Controls

In most cases, the button for turning a tablet on and off is located on the side of the body of the device, as are the other buttons and ports that can be used for various functions on your tablet.

On/Off button. This can also be used to put the tablet into Sleep mode. Press and hold for a couple of seconds to turn on the tablet. Press once to put it to sleep or wake it up from sleep.

Volume button. Press at the ends to increase or decrease volume.

Camera. This is the main, front-facing, camera for taking pictures.

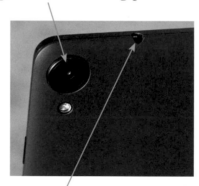

Headphone jack. This is used to attach a set of headphones.

Micro USB port. This can be used to attach the tablet to an adapter for charging, or to a computer for charging or to download content from the tablet, using the supplied USB cable.

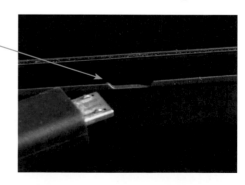

Setting Up Your Tablet

When you first turn on your tablet (by pressing and holding the On/Off button) you will be taken through the setup process. This only has to be done once, and some of the steps can be completed or amended at a later time, usually within the **Settings** app. Some of the elements that can be applied during the setup process are:

- **Language**. This option lets you select the language to use for your tablet. Whichever language is selected will affect all of the system text on the tablet, and it will also apply to all user accounts on the tablet.

- **Wi-Fi**. This can be used to set up your Wi-Fi connection so that you can access the web and online services. In the **Select Wi-Fi** window, tap on the name of your router. Enter the password for your router and tap on the **Connect** button.

- **Google Account**. At this stage you can create a Google Account, or sign in with an existing one. Once you have done this, you will have full access to the Google Account services and you will not have to enter your login details again.

- **Apps & data**. This option can be used to set up your new tablet from a backup that you have made on another device. This will include all of the apps and settings that you have on the other device. You can also set up your tablet as a new device.

- **Google services**. This includes options for the Google services that you want to use, including backing up your tablet, using location services and sending feedback to Google.

- **Google Feeds**. This is the personal news and feed function that can be used to display a range of cards with the information that is most important to you (see pages 52-56).

Don't forget

Most routers require a password when they are accessed for the first time by a new device. This is a security measure to ensure that other people cannot gain unauthorized access to your router and Wi-Fi.

Adding Accessories

As with most electrical gadgets, there is a wide range of accessories that can be used with Android tablets. Some of these are more cosmetic, while others provide useful additional functionality. Some to consider are:

- **Docking station**. This can be attached to your tablet and it doubles as a stand for viewing content, and also for charging your tablet.

- **Stylus pen**. This is a pen with a rubber tip that can be used to write on a tablet, tap on items to activate them, and also swipe between screens or pages.

- **Battery charging pack**. This is a mobile unit that can be used to charge your tablet when you are away from a mains source of power. The pack is charged initially (indicator lights show how much charge is available) and it can then be plugged into the tablet to give it additional power.

- **Cover**. This can be used to protect the tablet and, in some cases, double as a stand for viewing content on the tablet.

- **Screen protector**. If you want to give your tablet's screen extra protection, these sheets of clear plastic are a good option. Some of them also come with cleaning cloths.

- **USB adapter**. This is an adapter that connects to your tablet's micro USB connector so that USB devices can be connected to it. This can include digital cameras, pen drives and card readers for photos.

- **Mobile Wi-Fi unit**. This is a unit that can provide Wi-Fi access when you are away from your own Wi-Fi router. They are used with pay-as-you-go SIM cards so you only pay for what you use and do not need to have a long-term contract.

When you are buying accessories for your tablet, make sure that they are compatible with your device in terms of make and model.

Another useful accessory is a Bluetooth keyboard, which usually comes with a cover that acts as a stand for the tablet. It can be connected using the Bluetooth option in the Settings app.

2 Getting Started with Your Tablet

The interface on an Android tablet is more similar to that of a smartphone than a traditional computer. However, it also has many similar features to a computer and can perform a lot of the same tasks. This chapter details the Android interface and shows how to find your way around the Home screen, add apps and widgets, use settings and lock your tablet.

30 Viewing the Home Screen

31 Navigating Around

32 Adding Apps

33 Moving Apps

34 Working with Favorites

35 Adding Widgets

36 Changing the Background

37 Creating Folders

38 Using Notifications

40 Screen Rotation

41 Accessing Settings

44 Quick Settings

45 Editing Quick Settings

46 Locking Your Tablet

48 Searching

51 Ok Google

52 Using Google Feeds

Hot tip

There is also a **Quick Settings** area that can be accessed by swiping down from the top of the screen. See page 44 for more details.

Viewing the Home Screen

Once you have set up your tablet the first screen that you see will be the Home screen. This is also where you will return to when you tap the Home button from an app (see next page). The elements of the Home screen are:

Notifications Bar   Google Search box

Home screen area. This is where the majority of your commonly-used apps and widgets will be located

Favorites Tray

Navigation buttons   All Apps button

On different models of Android tablet, the Navigation buttons and All Apps button may be located in a slightly different position. The appearance of the Home screen may also be slightly different, depending on which apps the manufacturer wants to appear by default on the Home screen.

Navigating Around

At the bottom of the Home screen there are three buttons that can be used to navigate around your tablet. These appear on all subsequent pages that you visit so that you can always use them for navigation purposes.

The Navigation buttons are:

Back. Tap on this button to go back to the most recently-visited page or screen.

Home. Tap on this button to go back to the most recently-viewed Home screen at any point.

Recent Items. Tap on this to view the apps that you have used most recently. Tap on one of the apps to access it again. Swipe an app to the right to close the app, or tap on the cross in the top right-hand corner of the app.

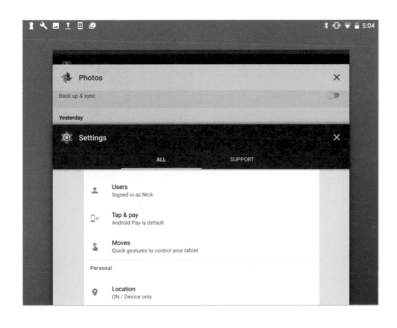

Most Android tablets have several Home screens. Swipe left and right to move between them.

31

When the keyboard is being used, the Back button turns into a down-pointing arrow. Tap on this once to hide the keyboard and reveal the Back button again.

Adding Apps

The Home screen is where you can add and manage your apps. To do this:

1 Tap on the **All Apps** button

2 All of the built-in apps are displayed. Tap on an app to open it

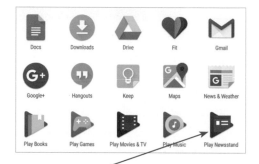

3 To add an app to the Home screen, press and hold on it

4 The Home screen will appear. Drag the app onto the screen on which you want it to be added, and release it

5 The app is added to the Home screen

6 Swipe left and right to move between the available Home screens

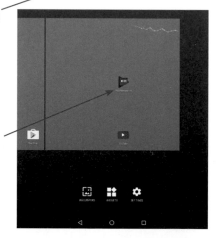

Moving Apps

Once apps have been added to the Home screen they can be repositioned and moved to other Home screens. To do this:

1 Press and hold on an app to move it. Drag it into its new position. A light outline appears, indicating where the app will be positioned

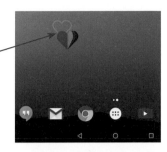

Don't forget

Apps can be moved to the left or right onto new Home screens.

2 Release the app to drop it into its new position

3 To move an app between Home screens, drag it to the edge of the Home screen

Beware

Make sure that the app is fully at the edge of the Home screen, otherwise it will not move to the next one. A thin, light border should appear just before it moves to the next Home screen.

4 As the app reaches the edge of the Home screen it will automatically move to the next one. Add it to the new Home screen in the same way as in Step 2

Don't forget

For some tablets, the Favorites Tray appears along the bottom of the screen in landscape mode. For others, it appears down the right-hand side of the screen.

Hot tip

Apps can appear in the **Favorites Tray** and also on individual Home screens, but they have to be added there each time from within the **All Apps** section.

Working with Favorites

The Favorites Tray at the bottom of the Home screen can be used to access the apps you use most frequently. This appears on all of the Home screens. Apps can be added to or removed from the Favorites Tray, as required.

1 Press and hold on an app in the **Favorites Tray** and drag it onto the Home screen.

A gap appears where the app has been removed

2 Tap and hold on any app in the **Favorites Tray** and

drag it into a new position as required

3 Press and hold on an app on the Home screen and drag it

onto a space in the **Favorites Tray** to add it there

4 The **Favorites Tray** has a limit to the number of apps that it can contain (usually six, plus the All Apps button), and if you try to add more than this, the app will spring back to its original location

Adding Widgets

Android widgets are similar to apps, except that they generally display specific content or real-time information. For instance, a photo gallery widget can be used to display photos directly on a Home screen, and a traffic widget can display updated information about traveling conditions. Widgets can be added from any Home screen:

1 Press and hold on an empty area on any Home screen and tap on the **Widgets** button

2 Swipe up and down to view all of the available widgets

3 Press and hold on a widget and drop it onto a Home screen as required, in the same way as for adding apps

Widget icons on the Home screen usually appear larger than those for standard apps.

Don't forget

Changing the Background

The background (wallpaper) for all of the Home screens on your tablet can be changed within the **Settings** app (**Settings** > **Display** > **Wallpaper**). However, it can also be changed directly from any Home screen. To do this:

1 Press and hold on an empty area on any Home screen and tap on the **Wallpapers** button

2 Tap on one of the options from where you would like to select the background wallpaper

3 Select a background and tap on the **Set wallpaper** button

4 Select whether the background is for the Home screen, the Lock screen, or both

5 The selected background is applied to all Home screens

Wallpaper apps can be downloaded from the Play Store, to add a wider range of backgrounds to your tablet. Enter '**wallpaper**' into the Search box of the **Apps** section of the Play Store (see pages 76-77).

Creating Folders

As you start to use your Android tablet for more activities, you will probably acquire more and more apps. These will generally be for a range of tasks covering areas such as productivity, communications, music, photos, business, and so on. Initially it may be easy to manage and access these apps, but as the number of them increases, it may become harder to locate and keep track of them all.

One way in which you can manage your apps is to create folders for apps covering similar subjects, e.g. one for productivity apps, one for entertainment apps, etc. To create folders for different apps:

To remove an app from a folder, press and hold on it and drag it out of the folder onto a Home screen.

1 Press and hold on an app and drag it over another one

2 Release the app. A folder will be created, containing both of the apps

3 Tap on a folder to view its contents. Initially it will be unnamed

4 Tap here and give the folder a relevant name

Adding folders to the Favorites Tray is a good way to make a larger number of apps available here, rather than the standard six permitted.

5 Folders can contain numerous items and also be placed in the **Favorites Tray**, in which case the folder name is not displayed

Using Notifications

Android tablets have numerous ways of keeping you informed; from new emails and calendar events, to the latest information about apps that have been downloaded and installed. To make it easier to view these items, they are grouped together in the Notifications area. This appears on the Lock Screen and can also be accessed from any Home screen from the Notifications bar.

Hot tip

Settings for the Notifications area can be applied in **Settings** > **Notifications**. These can be used to specify what is shown when the tablet is locked, and to select notifications for specific apps.

1 By default, notifications are shown on the Lock Screen. Tap on a notification here to access it directly

2 On any Home screen, notifications are indicated on the Notifications bar

3 Swipe down from the top of any Home screen to access your notifications. Some of these may display more details than on the Lock Screen

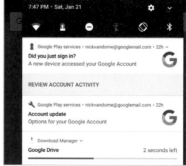

4 Tap on a notification to view its full details, within the relevant app, e.g. open Gmail to view new emails

Don't forget

Tap on the **Clear All** button to clear all of the current notifications. If you clear the notifications it does not delete the items; they remain within their relevant apps and can be viewed there.

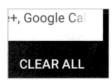

Grouped notifications

In Android 7.0 Nougat, notifications from apps are grouped together so that you can view them all at the same time in the

Notifications panel, and action them accordingly.

Replying to notifications

Also, for some apps such as those for messaging, it is possible to reply directly to a notification without opening the specific app.

Notifications Quick Settings

In Android 7.0 Nougat it is possible to apply quick notifications settings to an app directly from the Notifications panel, so that you can manage how specific apps use notifications, without having to go into the Settings app. To do this:

1 Press and hold on a notification in the Notifications panel

2 Tap on one of the options for how you want notifications from the app to operate

3 Tap on the **Done** button to apply the selection in Step 2, or tap on the **More Settings** button to access the notification options in the Settings app

Grouped notifications is a new feature in Android 7.0 Nougat.

Replying directly to notifications is a new feature in Android 7.0 Nougat.

Tap on the **Reply to** button to reply to a notification from an app such as Hangouts or Skype. A text box appears, into which you can type your message and send it.

Notifications Quick Settings is a new feature in Android 7.0 Nougat.

Screen Rotation

By default, the content on a tablet's screen rotates as you rotate the device. This means that the content can be viewed in portrait or landscape mode, depending on what is being used, e.g. for movies it may be preferable to have it in landscape mode, while for reading it may be better in portrait mode:

 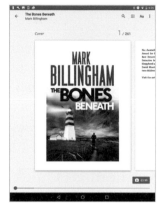

Don't forget

Screen rotation is achieved by a gyroscope sensor in the tablet.

It is also possible to lock the screen so that it does not rotate when you move it. This can be useful if you are using it for a specific task and do not want to be distracted by the screen rotating if you move your hand slightly. To lock and unlock the screen rotation:

1 Drag down twice from the top of the screen to access the **Quick Settings** (see page 44)

2 Tap on the **Auto-rotate** button to lock screen rotation

3 Tap on the **Portrait** button to disable the screen lock and return to Auto-rotate mode

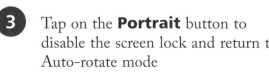

Accessing Settings

We all like to think of ourselves as individuals, and this extends to the appearance and operation of our electronic gadgets. An Android tablet offers a range of settings so that you can set it up exactly the way that you want and give it your own look and feel. These are available from the **Settings** app.

To access the **Settings** on your Android tablet:

1 Tap on the **All Apps** button

2 Tap on the **Settings** app

3 The full range of settings is displayed

4 Tap on an item to view all of the options for it (if necessary, tap on the options at the next level down to see their own options). Most options will have an On/Off button, a radio button or a checkbox to tick or untick

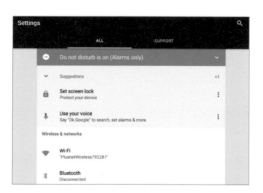

Hot tip

Add the **Settings** app to the **Favorites Tray** so that it is always quickly available.

Don't forget

Some settings may differ slightly between manufacturers but they will be broadly similar to those here. The settings shown here are for Android 7.0.

Don't forget

A radio button is round and appears with a dot inside it when it is selected; a checkbox is square and appears with a tick inside it when it is selected.

41

The Airplane mode, NFC and Network settings reset options are available from the **More** button in the Wireless & networks sections. NFC stands for Near Field Communication and is a set of standards used for devices whereby they can communicate with each other using radio waves once they are touched together.

Android Nougat has a new **Doze** function aimed at saving battery power. After the tablet has been inactive for a period of time it puts it into a deeper state of sleep than the standard sleep mode, to save power.

...cont'd

Wireless & networks

These settings are:

- **Wi-Fi**. Used for turning Wi-Fi on and off on your tablet and connecting to a router.

- **Bluetooth**. Used for connecting wirelessly to other Bluetooth-enabled devices over short distances.

- **Data usage**. Used to view how much data you have downloaded.

- **Airplane mode**. Check this on when taking a flight. It switches off all wireless activity, including cellular phone, SMS messages, Wi-Fi and Bluetooth functions.

- **NFC**. Used to swap content between compatible devices by touching them back-to-back.

- **Android Beam**. Used together with NFC to transfer content, such as photos.

- **Network settings reset**. This can be used to reset the network settings for Wi-Fi, cellular data and Bluetooth.

Device

These settings are:

- **Display**. Used to set the screen brightness, wallpaper and screen saver.

- **Notifications**. This can be used to choose which apps can provide notifications in the Notifications panel.

- **Sound**. This can be used to turn on or off the sounds used for the touchscreen, the Lock screen and docking.

- **Apps**. Used to show information about the installed apps on the tablet.

- **Storage**. Shows what is using up the storage space on the tablet and how much is being used.

- **Battery**. Shows what is using up the battery power.

- **Memory**. This shows how much memory has been used.

- **Users**. Used to show the users and add more as needed.

- **Tap & pay**. This can be used to set up and use Android Pay, which is a method of contactless payment that can be done with an Android device once an applicable debit or credit card has been registered.

- **Moves**. This contains options for quick gestures to control certain functions on the tablet.

Personal

These settings are:

- **Location**. Used to specify whether apps can use GPS and Wi-Fi on your tablet to identify its location.

- **Security**. A range of security settings for locking the tablet, encrypting its content and password details.

- **Accounts**. The Accounts settings can be used to add both Google and other accounts to your tablet.

- **Google**. This contains options for managing your Google Account and also some of the Google services.

- **Language & input**. Used to specify the system language for the tablet and also spelling and dictionary options.

- **Backup & reset**. This can be used to back up the data on your tablet or reset it to its factory settings.

System

These settings are:

- **Date & time**. Used to set your tablet's date and time.

- **Accessibility**. Settings that can be applied for users with visual or motor difficulties.

- **Printing**. Settings for saving compatible documents to the Google Drive (an online cloud storage service) so that they can be printed from there.

- **About tablet**. This displays details about your tablet.

If you reset your tablet to its factory settings, make sure that you have backed up its data first, as this will be cleared when the reset is performed (see page 160).

Cloud storage involves saving data on hardware in a remote physical location, which can be accessed from any device via the internet.

The **About tablet** (or **About device**) option under **System** displays the version of Android that is on your tablet.

Quick Settings

The full range of Android settings can be accessed from the Settings app. However, there is a Quick Settings option that can be accessed from the top of the screen. To use this:

1 Swipe down from the top of the screen to access the Notifications Area (see page 38)

2 Swipe down again from the top of the Notifications Area

3 The current **Quick Settings** options are displayed

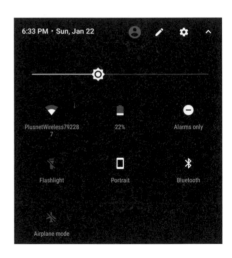

Hot tip

The Quick Settings can be accessed if the tablet is locked, but only with the Swipe method (see page 46 for details).

4 Tap on a setting to access its options in the **Settings** app, or

5 Tap on an item to apply it directly within **Quick Settings**. This can be done with **Airplane Mode**, **Auto-rotate** and **Brightness**. The **Brightness** option activates a separate widget that can be used to set the screen brightness

Editing Quick Settings

In Android Nougat, the Quick Settings area can be edited so that you have the exact items there that you want.

1 Access the Quick Settings area as shown on the previous page

Editing Quick Settings is a new feature in Android 7.0 Nougat.

2 Tap on this button to **Edit** the Quick Settings area

3 The edit area has two panels: the top panel contains the current Quick Settings, with the additional ones in the panel below

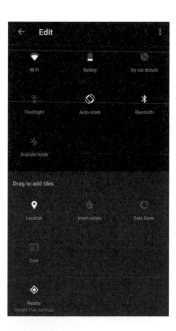

4 Drag items from the bottom panel into the top panel, and vice versa, to customize the items in the Quick Settings area

5 Tap on this button to apply the editing changes and return to the Quick Settings area which is amended accordingly

Locking Your Tablet

Security is an important issue for any computing device, and this applies to physical security as much as online security. For Android tablets it is possible to place a digital lock on the screen, so that only an authorized user can open it. This is useful when there are several user accounts on the same tablet. There are different ways in which a lock can be set:

1 Tap on the **Settings** app

Settings

2 In the **Personal** section, tap on the **Security** option

🔒 Security

3 The current method of **Screen lock** is displayed here. Tap on this to access the options

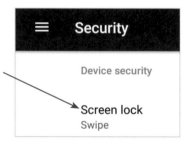
≡ Security

Device security

Screen lock
Swipe

Beware

The Swipe option is only really useful for avoiding items being activated accidentally when your tablet is not in use; it is not a valid security method. The most secure method is a password containing letters, numbers and characters.

4 The methods for locking the screen are **None**, **Swipe**, **Pattern**, **PIN** and **Password**. Tap on the required method to select it and set its attributes

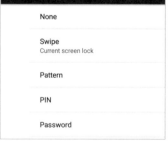
← Choose screen lock

None

Swipe
Current screen lock

Pattern

PIN

Password

5 The **Swipe** option is the least secure (after **None**) as it only requires the padlock icon to be swiped to the edge of the circle to unlock the tablet. No other security authorization is required

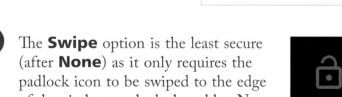

6 For the **PIN** (or **Password**) option, enter the PIN in the box and tap on the **Continue** button. Enter the PIN again for confirmation. This will then need to be entered whenever you want to unlock the tablet

Whenever your tablet goes to sleep it will need to be unlocked before you can use it again. Sleep mode can be activated by pressing the **On**/**Off** button once. After a period of inactivity the tablet will also go into Sleep mode automatically: the length of time until this happens can be specified within **Settings** > **Display** > **Sleep**.

47

7 For the **Pattern** option, drag over the keypad to create the desired pattern, then press Continue and enter again to confirm

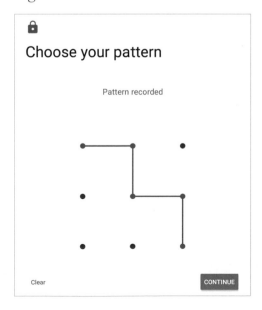

Searching

Since Android is owned by Google, it is unsurprising that tablets with this operating system come with the power of Google's search functionality. Items can be searched for on the tablet itself, or on the web. This can be done by typing in the Google Search box and also by using the voice search option. To search for items on an Android tablet:

1 By default, in both portrait

and landscape mode, the Google Search box appears at the top of every Home screen

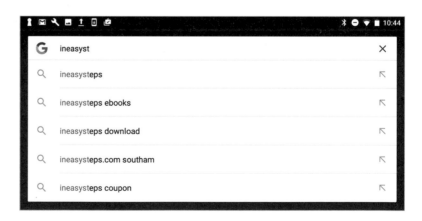

2 Tap within it and begin typing a word or phrase. As you type, corresponding suggestions will appear, both for on the web and for apps on the tablet

On some tablets, the search option is indicated by a magnifying glass with the word Google next to it.

3 As you continue to type, the suggestions will become more defined

4 Tap on an app result to open it directly on your tablet, or tap on this button on the keyboard to view the results from the web

Voice search

To use the voice search functionality on your tablet, instead of typing a search query:

1 Tap on the microphone button in the Search box or if set up, say "Ok Google" (see page 51)

2 When the microphone button turns red, speak the word or phrase for which you want to search

49

3 You can use voice search to find or open items on your tablet or from the web. On your tablet you can use voice search to open apps, such as the Gmail app

open Gmail

4 The app opens in the same way as if you had tapped on it from the Home screen

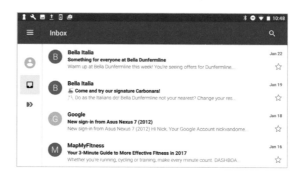

Don't forget

The phrase displayed in the voice search window is sometimes a summary of what you actually say. For instance, if you say "**Please open Gmail app**" the words "**open gmail**" may be displayed.

5 If you search for items on the web, Google will use your location and also your search history to give you more accurate results, for instance if you search for 'Indian restaurants' it will display the results for those closest to your location

Ok Google

The latest version of Google Search on Android has a voice search function that can be activated by saying "Ok Google" from any screen. You can then speak your search query as shown on pages 49-50. To use Ok Google:

1 The Ok Google prompt appears in the Search box, but it has to be set up before it can be used

2 Open the Google Search app and tap on the **Get Started** button

GET STARTED

It may take Ok Google longer to recognize regional accents, but it should identify them after a bit of practice.

51

3 Train your tablet to recognize your voice by saying "Ok Google" three times

4 Tap on the **Finish** button to complete the setup for Ok Google. This can now be used from any screen on your tablet

Using Google Feeds

We live in an age where we want the availability of as much up-to-date information as possible. On an Android tablet, one option for this is Google Feeds. This is a digital assistant service that provides items such as the latest traffic information for your area, flight information or the results from your favorite sports team. The information displayed is tailored to your needs according to your location and the type of content that you access.

When Google Feeds is activated this also turns on your location history so that Google can make use of the location data that is collected by your tablet.

Google Feeds cards
The functionality of Google Feeds is provided by cards. These display up-to-date information for a variety of topics. You can apply your own specific settings for each card and these will then display new information as it occurs. Cards appear when it is deemed that they are necessary, based on your location. So, if you are traveling in a different country, you will see a different range of cards from those when you are at home. Some of the most popular default cards include those for traveling to specific destinations (such as work), and sports cards.

To use Google Feeds on your tablet you have to be connected to the internet via Wi-Fi.

Google Feeds was previously known as Google Now and some of this terminology remains in the app.

The Google Feeds page can be accessed from the Google app in Step 1 on the next page and also by swiping inwards from the left-hand edge of the screen.

Accessing Google Feeds

By default, Google Feeds is not automatically on (although it can be turned on during the initial setup process for your tablet). To activate it so that it works for you in the background:

1 Tap on the **Google** app

2 Tap on the **Set Up** button at the bottom of the screen

SET UP

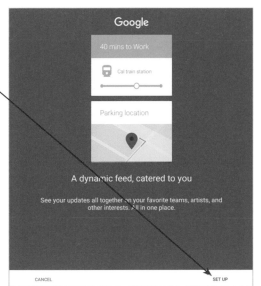

3 Tap on the **Yes, I'm In** button on the **Set up the feed?** page

YES, I'M IN

Set up the feed?

To get the feed, you need to have the following Google Account settings turned on for nickvandome@googlemail.com:

Your searches and browsing activity

Web & App Activity includes searches, Chrome history, and content you browse on the web and in apps

Information from your devices

Device Information includes contacts, calendars, apps, music, battery life, sensor readings

Google Feeds also accesses your web history, in order to provide you with as much relevant information as possible. This is stored as part of your Google Account and can be accessed by logging in with your account details at the website **accounts.google.com** and accessing the **My Activity** section.

Some of the Google Feeds cards include: weather, traffic, sports, public transport, appointments, news updates, stocks and travel. There is also a range of Gmail cards that can be used to track items that have been bought online where Gmail has been used for the confirmation email, such as packages, restaurant bookings and flights.

...cont'd

Around Google Feeds

When you first activate Google Feeds you will see the Home screen. This is where your cards will show up and where you can access all of the settings for individual cards, such as selecting the frequency of updates, customization, and how details are displayed.

Don't forget

The Google Search box is located at the top of the Google Feeds Home screen. This can be used to search your Google Feeds cards, your tablet and also the web.

Hot tip

To delete a card, swipe it left or right off the screen. The card will come back the next time that the item is updated.

1 Active cards are shown on the Home screen

2 Tap here to view the card's individual settings

3 Specific settings can be applied for individual cards, such as the way in which the weather card displays its information

Customizing Google Feeds

Google Feeds can be customized so that you get exactly the type of information that you want. To do this:

1 Tap on this button at the top of the Google Feeds window

2 Tap on the **Customize** button

Reminders

Customize

Settings

The **Settings** option in Step 2 provides a range of settings that can be applied for Google Search and also Google Feeds.

3 Tap on the items at the top of the window to specify the way in which directions are displayed

Customize the feed

Places

Perth, UK

15 County Pl, Perth PH2 8EE, UK

In your stream

Apps & websites

People

Places   2

Sports   2

4 Tap on the categories at the bottom of the window to add more cards, including those for Sport, Stocks, Places and TV & Movies

...cont'd

5 For the items in Step 4, tap on a category and tap on an option to add another card, such as **Add a team**

6 Enter the name of the required item. For some options, suggestions will appear as you type

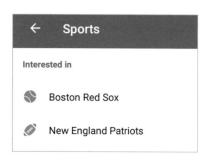

Add a team

new eng

New Eng**land** **Patriots**

New Eng**land** **Revolution**

Beware

Only teams can be added from the Sports section on Google Feeds, not individual sports people.

7 The selected item is included as something in which you are interested

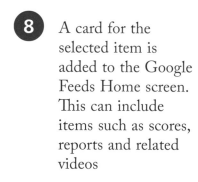

← **Sports**

Interested in

🎾 Boston Red Sox

🏈 New England Patriots

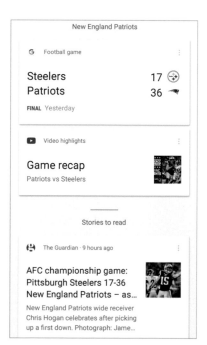

New England Patriots

G Football game ⋮

Steelers 17
Patriots 36

FINAL Yesterday

▶ Video highlights ⋮

Game recap
Patriots vs Steelers

——————

Stories to read

The Guardian · 9 hours ago ⋮

AFC championship game:
Pittsburgh Steelers 17-36
New England Patriots – as...

New England Patriots wide receiver
Chris Hogan celebrates after picking
up a first down. Photograph: Jame...

8 A card for the selected item is added to the Google Feeds Home screen. This can include items such as scores, reports and related videos

3 At Your Fingertips

*This chapter introduces
the touchscreen
keyboard and shows
how to add content
with it.*

58 The Android Keyboard

60 Keyboard Settings

62 Keyboard Shortcuts

64 Adding Text

65 Working with Text

66 Creating a Dictionary

The Android Keyboard

The keyboard on an Android tablet is a virtual one, i.e. it appears on the touchscreen whenever text or numbered input is required for an app. This can be for a variety of reasons:

- Entering text with a word processing app, email or a notes app.

- Entering a web address.

- Entering information into a form.

- Entering a username or password.

When you attempt one of the items above, the keyboard appears before you can enter any text or numbers:

Around the keyboard
To access the various keyboard controls:

1 Tap once on this button to add a single capital letter (the keyboard letters are displayed as capitals)

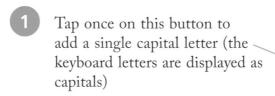

2 Double-tap on this button to create **Caps Lock**. This is indicated by a blue line underneath the arrow

3 Tap on this button to back-delete an item

4 Tap once on this button to access the **Numbers** keyboard option

5 From the Numbers keyboard, tap once on this button to access the **Symbols** keyboard

6 Tap once on this button on either of the two keyboards above to return to the standard **QWERTY** option

ABC

7 Tap once on this button to hide the keyboard (this can be done from the Navigation bar at the bottom of the screen).
If the keyboard is hidden, tap once on one of the input options, e.g. entering text, to show it again

Hot tip

If you are entering a password or details into a form, the keyboard will have a **Go** or **Send** button that can be used to activate the information that has been entered.

Keyboard Settings

There are a number of options for setting up the functionality of your Android tablet's keyboard. These can be accessed from the Personal section within Settings:

1 Open the **Settings** app and tap on the **Language & input** button under **Personal**

2 Tap here to enable the **Spell checker**

3 Tap on the **Virtual keyboard** option to access the settings for the default Google Keyboard, Gboard

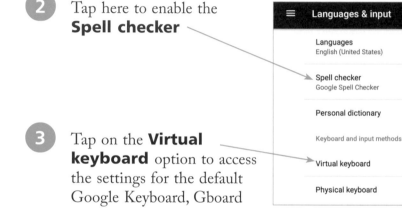

4 Tap on the **Gboard** button to access the settings for the default Google Keyboard

5 The options for the keyboard settings are listed in the left-hand panel

If the Spell checker is turned on, misspelled words will be underlined in red when they are entered with the keyboard.

6 Tap on the **Text correction** option and drag the buttons On or Off in the right-hand panel for each option, such as **Show suggestions** and **Auto-correction**

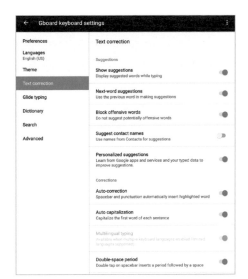

Tap the **Show suggestions** button On under **Text correction** to display suggested words as you type.

7 Drag the **Next-word suggestions** button **On** in Step 6, which helps to make a suggestion of the next word in the context of what is being written

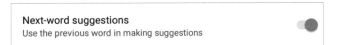

8 Tap on the **Advanced** button to access the advanced settings for the Google Keyboard, Gboard, including sending usage statistics to Google

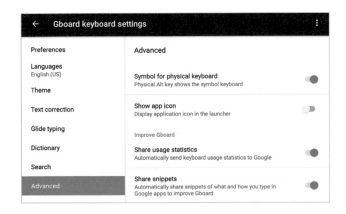

Keyboard Shortcuts

Because of the size of the keyboard on an Android tablet, some of the keys need to have duplicate functionality, in order to fit in all of the options. This includes keys with multiple options, accented letters and keyboard settings options.

Much of this functionality is accessed by pressing and holding on keys, rather than just tapping on them once.

Keyboard settings

To access the keyboard settings directly from the keyboard:

1 Press and hold on this button

2 Tap on the **Settings** button

3 Tap on **Input options > Languages** or **Gboard keyboard settings** to access the full range of settings for the keyboard

Dual functions

If a key has more than one character on it, both items can be accessed from the same button.

1 Tap on a button to insert the main character

2 Press and hold on the button to access the second character (visible in the top right-hand corner of the key). Release the button to insert the character

Don't forget

Some tablets may have their own keyboard settings, but they are similar to those for the Google Keyboard, Gboard.

Accented letters

Specific letters on the keyboard can also be used to include accented letters for words in different languages.

1 Press and hold on a letter that has corresponding accented versions used in different languages. Tap on a letter to insert it

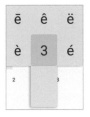

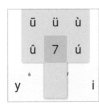

The accented letters are available on the keyboard regardless of which language dictionaries are installed.

2 The **Return** key also has a **Previous** button that can be accessed by pressing and holding on it. This can be used when filling in online forms

Spacebar shortcut

The spacebar also has a useful shortcut: at the end of a sentence, double-tap on the spacebar to add a full stop/period and a space, ready for the start of the next sentence. This can be specified within **Gboard keyboard settings** > **Preferences**.

Numbers can be added from the Numbers keyboard and also by pressing and holding on the top line of the QWERTY keyboard and swiping over a number.

Double-space period
Double tap on spacebar inserts a period followed by a space

Adding Text

Once you have applied the keyboard settings that you require, you can start entering text. To do this:

1 Tap once on the screen to activate the keyboard. Start typing with the keyboard. The text will appear at the point where you tapped on the screen

Hot tip

If you do not want to use the underlined auto-correction word, tap on one of the others on the bar above the keyboard. Tap on it again to save the word to your own custom dictionary, so that auto-correction will remember it the next time you want to use it.

2 If **Auto-correction** is enabled, suggestions appear above the keyboard. Tap once on the spacebar to accept the suggestion, or tap on another word to insert that instead

3 If the **Spell checker** is enabled, any misspelled words appear underlined in red

She was very sucessful

4 Tap on a misspelled word to view suggested alternatives. Tap on one to replace the misspelled word or delete it

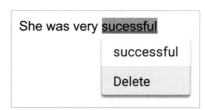

Working with Text

Once text has been entered it can be selected, copied, cut and pasted, either within an app or between apps.

Selecting text

To select text and perform tasks on it:

1 Tap anywhere to set the insertion point for adding or editing text

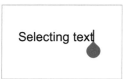

2 Drag the marker to move the insertion point

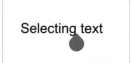

3 Double-tap on a word to activate the selection handles

4 Drag the handles to change the text that is selected

5 Tap on these buttons at the top of the window to **Cut** or **Copy** the selected text

6 Locate the point at which you want to include the text. Press and hold and tap on **Paste** to add the text

There is usually a **Paste** option on the main toolbar of apps in which you want to paste text that has been copied.

Creating a Dictionary

In addition to the standard dictionaries on your Android tablet it is also possible to create your own custom dictionary. This could include real names, or words which you use regularly but do not appear in the virtual dictionary. To create your own dictionary:

Do not use a shortcut that is an actual word, otherwise it could cause confusion.

1 Access **Settings** > **Language & input** > and tap on the **Personal dictionary** button

2 At this point the dictionary will be empty. Tap on the **Add** button to create an entry

3 Enter the word or phrase, and a shortcut with which to access it. Tap on this arrow on the keyboard

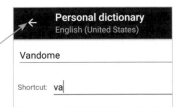

4 Tap on this button on the keyboard. The entry is added to your custom dictionary

5 When entering text, enter the shortcut. The word will appear on the options bar above the keyboard. Tap on the required word to insert it

4 Working with Apps

Apps on an Android tablet are the programs that provide its functionality. This chapter details the built-in ones, and shows how to download more and update them.

68 About Android Apps

69 Built-in Apps

72 Multitasking with Apps

74 Around the Play Store

76 Finding Apps

78 Downloading Apps

80 Deleting Apps

81 Updating Apps

82 App Information

About Android Apps

An app is just a more modern name for a computer program. The terminology first became widely used on smartphones, but has now spread to all forms of computing and is firmly embedded in the language of tablets.

On Android tablets there are two types of apps:

- **Built-in apps**. These are the apps that come pre-installed on your Android tablet.

- **Play Store apps**. These are apps that can be downloaded from the online Play Store.

Using apps

To use apps on an Android tablet:

In addition to the Play Store, some tablet manufacturers also offer their own app stores, although the range of apps is usually more limited.

1 The full range of Android apps can be viewed by tapping on the **All Apps** button

2 Tap once on an app to open it

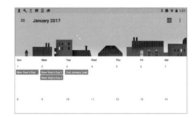

3 Tap on either of the **Menu** buttons to access individual settings for a specific app

Built-in Apps

The built-in apps that are available from the All Apps screen can vary slightly depending on the brand of Android tablet being used. However, some of the generic apps should include:

- **Calculator**. A standard calculator that also has some scientific functions, although not the range of a full scientific calculator.
  Calculator

- **Calendar**. An app for storing appointments, important dates and other calendar information. It can be synced with your Google Account.
  Calendar

- **Chrome**. Different Android tablets have different types of browsers for accessing the web. The Chrome browser is the default on some tablets.
  Chrome

- **Clock**. This can be used to view the time in different countries and also as an alarm clock and a stopwatch.
  Clock

- **Contacts**. This is the Android address book where you can enter contact details for your friends and family members. It can also be synced with your Google Account.
  Contacts

- **Docs**. This can be used to create word processing documents and keep them in cloud storage (online storage) or on your tablet.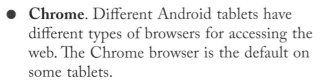
  Docs

- **Downloads**. When you download content onto your tablet it can be viewed and managed in this app. It can also be used to view web pages offline.
  Downloads

- **Drive**. This is another Google app and provides online storage and backup for documents and files on your tablet.
  Drive

...cont'd

- **Fit**. This is an app for monitoring and recording your fitness activities. You can set your own goals and check your progress against them.

Fit

- **Gmail**. When you set up a Google Account you will also create a Gmail account for sending and receiving email. This app can be used for accessing and using your Gmail.

Gmail

- **Google**. This app can be used for accessing the Google Search function, still one of the best search facilities available. It can also be used for accessing the Google feeds function, if set up.

Google

- **Google+**. This can be used with your Google Account to share content such as photos and updates with specific people.

Google+

- **Keep**. This is like a digital pinboard where you can add notes, reminders and lists.

Keep

- **Hangouts**. This is a Google social media app that can be used to chat with friends using either text or video and share photos.

Hangouts

- **Maps**. Google's Maps app is one of the best mapping apps available for finding locations and obtaining directions.

Maps

- **Photos**. This is the default Android app for viewing, managing and sharing your photos.

Photos

- **Play Books**. This is the app for reading ebooks on an Android tablet. It can be used to manage books in your library and also download new ones from the Play Store.

Play Books

Hot tip

Messages from the Hangouts app can be replied to directly from the Notification area, without having to first open the app.

- **Play Games**. This is the app for accessing games from the Play Store and playing them on your tablet.

Play Games

- **Play Movies & TV**. Another app linked to the Play Store. It is used to view movies that you have bought or rented from the Play Store and to view your own personal videos.

Play Movies & TV

- **Play Music**. This is the default music player that can be used to play your own music and also music content from the Play Store.

Play Music

Don't forget

Some Android tablets have different apps for functions such as playing music and movies and reading books and magazines. If this is the case, the Play apps here can still be downloaded from the Play Store.

- **Play Newsstand**. Similar to the Play Books app, this is used for reading news and magazines and downloading new ones from the Play Store.

Play Newsstand

- **Play Store**. This is where all of the online content for Android tablets can be accessed, bought and downloaded. This includes apps, books, music, movies and magazines.

Play Store

- **Settings**. This contains all of the settings that can be applied to the tablet to customize it to the way you want. It is good idea to add it to the Favorites Tray for quick access from any Home screen.

Settings

- **Sheets**. This can be used to create spreadsheets and keep them in cloud storage (online storage) or on your tablet.

Sheets

- **Slides**. This can be used to create presentations and keep them in cloud storage (online storage) or on your tablet.

Slides

- **YouTube**. This provides direct access to the popular video sharing website.

YouTube

Multitasking with Apps

When using a tablet it is sometimes useful to be able to view two windows side-by-side on the screen. Android Nougat introduces this functionality, known as multitasking.

Being able to view two apps in the same window is a new feature in Android 7.0 Nougat.

Pressing and holding on a button is also known as a long press.

1 Open an app and press and hold on the **Recent Items** button

2 The app being used is shown in the left-hand panel. The recently used apps are in the right-hand panel

3 Tap on one of the apps in the right-hand panel to make it active. Each app can be used independently of the other

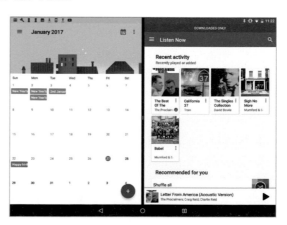

Once multitasking has been activated, the Recent items button changes into the Multitasking button.

72

4 Tap on the Home button to return to the Home screen

5 The apps in the multitasking view are minimized at the side of the screen. Tap on another app to make it active in the multitasking window

Press on the Multitasking button to view the recently viewed apps in the right-hand panel, as in Step 2. Tap on an app to make it active in the right-hand panel.

Hot tip

6 The newly selected app is available in the multitasking window

NEW

7 Drag on this bar to change the amount of the screen each app takes up

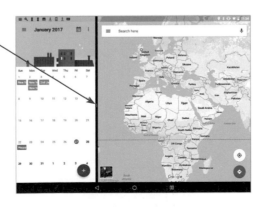

In normal view, double-tap on the **Recent Items** button to toggle between the two most recently used apps. This is known as **Quick Switch**.

Hot tip

Around the Play Store

Although the built-in apps provide a lot of useful functionality and are a good starting point, the Play Store is where you can really start to take advantage of the wide range of apps that are available. These can be used for entertainment, communication, productivity and much more.

To access the Play Store and find apps:

Don't forget

New apps are added to the Play Store on a regular basis (and existing ones are updated) so the Homepage will change appearance regularly.

1. Tap on the **Play Store** app

2. Suggested items are shown on the Play Store Homepage

Don't forget

App prices are shown in the local currency.

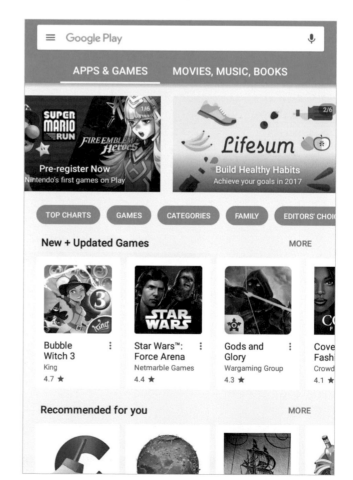

3 Swipe up and down to see the full range of recommendations, for all types of content in the Play Store. Tap on an item to view further details about it

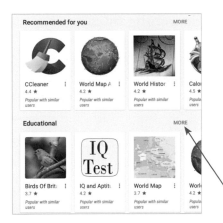

Tap on the **More** button in a section on the Homepage to view additional items.

4 Use these buttons to find content according to **Apps & Games** or **Movies, Music, Books**

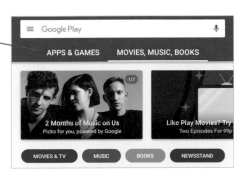

5 Tap on the **Menu** button to access the Play Store menu

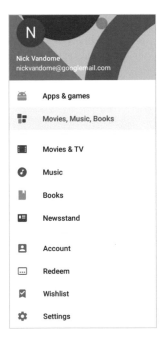

If you have a Play Store Gift Card, it can be redeemed from the **Redeem** button, which can be accessed from the Menu button at the top of the Play Store window. Enter the Gift Card code and the relevant amount will be credited to your Google Play balance for use in the Play Store.

75

Finding Apps

Searching by category

When you have accessed the Apps section of the Play Store you can then look for content in a variety of ways:

There may be different apps available in the Play Store depending on your geographical location.

1 The featured and recommended items are displayed on the Apps Homepage. Swipe up and down to view the full range and tap on an item to view more details

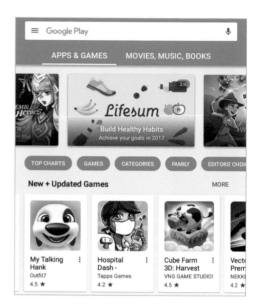

2 Swipe left and right on the top bar to view apps according to **Top Charts**, **Games**, **Categories**, **Family**, **Editors' Choice** and **Early Access**

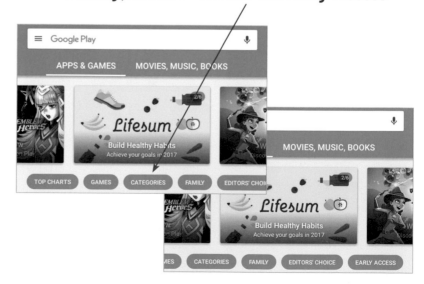

3 Tap on the **Categories** tab in Step 2 and tap on a category to view the apps according to these headings

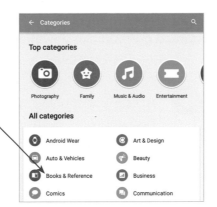

4 Search for apps within a category in the same way as for searching over the whole range of apps as in Step 2

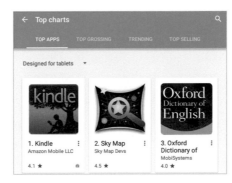

Using the Search box

1 Tap in the Search Google Play box on any page to conduct a search with keywords

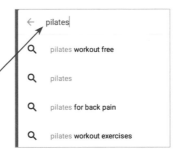

2 Enter the name of the item for which you want to search

3 Tap on one of the suggested results or tap on this button on the keyboard

As you type in the Search box, the suggested items will change, depending on the keyword(s) used.

Downloading Apps

Once you have found an app in the Play Store that you want to use, you can download it to your tablet:

1 Access the app you want to use. Tap here to view a video preview of the app (if available). There will also be details about the app and reviews from other users

Under **Settings** > **Notifications**, select apps to apply settings for their notifications in the Notifications Area.

78

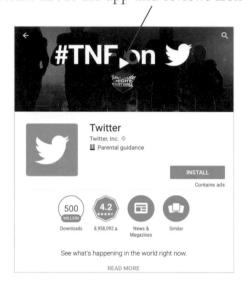

2 Tap on the **Install** button

INSTALL

3 Tap on the **Accept** button to accept the permissions requested by the app

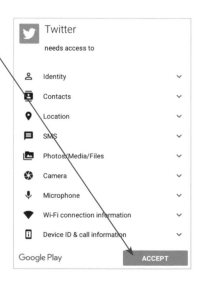

4 The progress of the download is shown on the Apps Homepage in the Play Store (and also in the Notifications Area)

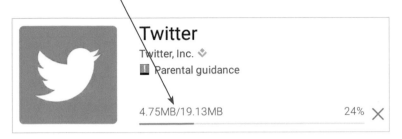

5 Newly downloaded apps are added where there is space on the next available Home screen

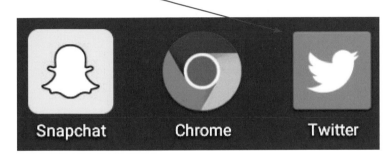

6 For a paid-for app, tap on the price button and tap on the **Accept** button as in Step 3 on the previous page. Tap on the **Open** button in the Play Store to open the app directly from here

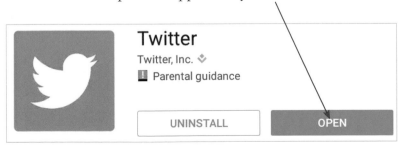

Hot tip

If you have a tablet with 3G/4G cellular capability, try downloading apps over Wi-Fi to avoid using too much of your data allowance.

79

Deleting Apps

The built-in apps on an Android tablet cannot be deleted easily, but the ones that have been downloaded from the Play Store can be removed. You may want to do this if you do not use a certain app any more and you feel the number of apps on your tablet is becoming unmanageable. To delete a downloaded app:

Don't forget

Drag the app over the **Remove** button in Step 1 to remove it from the Home screen. However, it is still available from the All Apps section. Built-in apps cannot be uninstalled, but they can be removed from the Home screen.

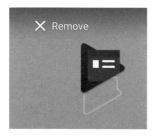

Don't forget

If apps have been deleted from the tablet, they can be reinstalled from the Play Store app by selecting **My apps & games** from the main menu and tapping on the **All** button to view all of the apps that have previously been downloaded.

1 Press and hold on one of the apps on the Home screen, until the Trash icon appears at the top. The **Remove** and **Uninstall** options are available

2 Drag the app over the **Uninstall** button until it turns red

3 Tap on the **OK** button to confirm the deletion

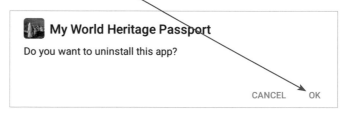

Updating Apps

The world of apps is a dynamic and fast-moving one, and new apps are being created and added to the Play Store on a daily basis. Existing apps are also being updated, to improve their performance and functionality. Once you have installed an app from the Play Store, it is possible to obtain updates at no extra cost (even if the app was paid for). To do this:

1 Access the Play Store. Tap on the **Menu** button and then the **My apps & games** button

Apps are also updated to improve security features and include any fixes to improve the performance of the app.

2 Tap on the **Installed** tab to view the apps on your tablet. Tap here to update all of the appropriate apps or tap on the **Update** button next to a specific app to update it

App Information

For both built-in apps and those downloaded from the Play Store it is possible to view details about them, and also see the permissions that they are using to access certain functions. To view information about your apps:

1 Open the **Settings** app and tap on the **Apps** button under **Device**

2 Tap on **All apps** and tap on an app

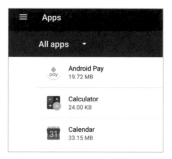

3 Tap on the **Force stop** button to close a running app

4 Details about the size of the app and the amount of data it has stored are shown here

5 Swipe down to **Permissions** to view which functions the app is accessing on your tablet

5 Useful Apps

Everyone has different interests and hobbies, and this chapter looks at a range of apps for a variety of topics.

84 Staying Organized

86 Being Productive

88 Keeping Entertained

90 Lifestyle

94 Health and Fitness

98 Family History

Staying Organized

Tablets offer a lot in terms of entertainment and communication, but they are also excellent for helping to keep us organized in our everyday lives, whether it is keeping notes, making to-do lists or even finding lost items in the dark. There are also options for organizing the tablet itself.

Evernote

One of the top note-taking options, this sophisticated and powerful app delivers functionality for creating notes that can then be viewed via Evernote on a variety of other devices, once you have created a new account. Photos, videos and audio clips can be added to notes.

Hot tip

Dropbox is a great way to store and share photos, particularly when you are traveling. If you have a Wi-Fi connection, you will be able to upload your photos while you are on vacation, which is a great way to keep them safe.

Dropbox

Storing content in the "cloud" is becoming increasingly common. This is the method of storing and sharing items on a company's computer server, rather than just on your own device. One of the best options is Dropbox, which provides

access to this method of sharing the content on your tablet. Once you have set up an account, which is free, you can upload content from your tablet that can then be accessed by yourself or other people from an internet-enabled device that has Dropbox installed, or via a web browser.

ColorNote Notepad Notes

A simple but effective note-taking app that can be used to jot down your thoughts, ideas or lists.

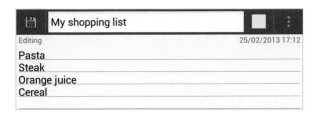

Better Note Notepad

Another simple, but effective, note-taking app.

Handrite Notes Notepad

A note-taking app that allows you to write the notes on the tablet's touchscreen, using either your finger or a stylus pen. It can take a bit of practice to get the handwriting looking its best, but it is worth persevering with.

Any.Do: To-do list & Reminders

A to-do list and task reminder app that can be used to organize your daily, weekly and monthly tasks. Items can be entered using text input or speech, and alerts can be set.

Flashlight

If you need to find or read something in the dark, this app can help light your way. Use either the tablet's camera or its screen as a flashlight.

All-in-One Toolbox (Cleaner)

An app for organizing your tablet. This can be used for a variety of housekeeping tasks, such as boosting system memory, a task killer for closing down unresponsive apps, and over a dozen other tools for optimizing the performance of your tablet.

Battery Widget

A handy app for displaying details about the performance of your tablet's battery.

A lot of apps have a Lite version and a Pro version. The Lite version is free, while there is usually a charge for the Pro version. Lite versions usually have restricted functionality compared with the Pro versions.

Being Productive

Traditional productivity tasks, such as creating letters or documents with word processing, or compiling spreadsheets for things like household expenses, are well catered for on Android tablets. There are versions of the popular Microsoft productivity apps such as Word, Excel and PowerPoint in the Play Store, and also a range of other apps that can open files in these formats and create them too.

Before downloading a productivity app, check the information about it in the Play Store to make sure that it can work with Microsoft documents, if that is what you want it for. All of the Play Store productivity apps can also be used on their own to create content on your tablet.

WPS Office (by Kingsoft)

A free office app that still manages to support the use of 23 different file types, including all of the popular Microsoft ones: Word, Excel and PowerPoint. Documents can be created using preset templates to ensure that they are created in a suitable format.

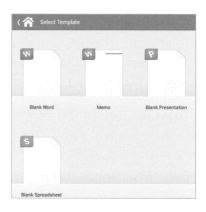

OfficeSuite Pro

A fully functioning suite of apps for word processing, spreadsheets, presentations and reading PDF documents. Aimed largely at the business user, it is still ideal for use in the home if you are going to be undertaking a range of productivity tasks.

Smart Office 2

Another office suite of apps that can be used to create, open and view Microsoft Office documents. It can also be used to print documents without the need for using a separate printing app (see next page).

Don't forget

Office suite apps usually have a File Manager functionality too, where you can view and manage the files that you have created with the app.

Writer

A basic word processing app, but one that can be used to create documents that are longer than those created with a notes app. When documents are created they are automatically saved by Writer, creating a document title with the first line that has been entered.

Simple Spreadsheet

As the name suggests, a simple app for creating spreadsheets. It does not have as much functionality as some of those with the suites of apps, but it can still be used for spreadsheets for items such as household expenditure or vacation expenses.

Mobile Print – PrinterShare

By default there is no option for printing from most Android apps. This app can be used to print documents wirelessly by sending them via Wi-Fi to your printer. To achieve this you will need to have a printer that is connected to your wireless network. Open the app and select the type of item that you want to print, and then select the required printer (which has to be turned on in order for the app to discover it wirelessly).

PrintHand Mobile Print

Another paid-for printing app that can be used to print documents, photos and emails.

Most printer manufacturers have their own apps that can be used to print on their own compatible printers.

There is a Lite version of the PrinterShare app. This only allows for printing test pages. If you want unlimited printing you will have to pay for the Premium version.

Some printer apps require you to download printer drivers to ensure that they can work with your installed printers. These are small programs that help the app and the printer talk to each other.

Keeping Entertained

There are a number of built-in Android apps that can be used for several areas of entertainment, such as reading, listening to music and watching movies. In addition, the Play Store also has hundreds of apps to add to your entertainment options.

Depending on your geographical location there will be other video subscription apps that you should be able to use.

Netflix

An app for the popular website for downloading and watching movies and TV shows on your tablet. A subscription is required for the service, and you can then search for and watch thousands of movies and TV shows.

IMDb Movies & TV

A comprehensive database of everything connected with movies and TV shows, including information about them, their stars and directors and clips from them. It is owned by Amazon and there are links for a lot of the items so that you can buy them directly from the Amazon website.

TuneIn Radio

Listen to digital radio on your tablet with this app. You can listen to stations from around the world, and search for content according to different categories such as music, sports, news, talk and location.

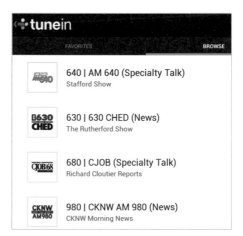

Social networking is now an important part of the online experience. Apps for Facebook and Twitter can be downloaded from the Play Store and used to communicate with family and friends, and provide entertainment opportunities through sharing photos and videos, and playing games. See pages 140-141 for more details.

Radio Online – PCRADIO

An eclectic range of radio stations, broadcasting on the internet around the world.

Magic Piano

A music app which can be used to download songs (from classical to pop) and then play along with them by following lightbeams on the virtual piano keyboard. A great way to learn the piano and play along with a variety of songs.

My Piano

Another Piano app with a virtual keyboard that can be used to learn the piano, or play your favorite tunes on your tablet if you are already a pianist.

Games

Although computer games may seem like the preserve of the younger generation, this is definitely not the case. Not all computer games are of the shoot-em-up or racing variety, and the Play Store also contains puzzles and versions of popular board games. Some games to try are:

As well as the games here, there is also a full range of other types of games in the Play Store. Two favorites are Candy Crush and Angry Birds.

- **Chess**. Pit your wits against a selection of free Chess apps. Various settings can be applied for each game, such as the level of difficulty.

- **Checkers**. Similar to the Chess apps, but for Checkers (Draughts). Hints are also available to help develop your skills and knowledge.

- **Mahjong**. A version of the popular Chinese game that can be used in single-player mode, and there are also options for linking up with other online players.

- **Solitaire**. An old favorite; the card game where you have to build sequences and remove all of the cards.

- **Sudoku**. The numbers game where you have to fill different grids with numbers 1-9, without having any of the same in a row or column.

- **Tetris**. One of the original computer games, where you have to piece together falling shapes to make lines.

- **Words With Friends**. Similar to Scrabble, an online word game, played with other users.

Lifestyle

When it comes to hobbies and pastimes, the Play Store has apps that cover a wide range of lifestyle options.

Gardeners Calendar

For anyone who is interested in the increasingly popular pastime of growing your own vegetables. All of the information is self-contained within the app and covers all aspects of growing vegetables, with details about what you need to do at different times of the year.

Most lifestyle topics have several apps covering them. Try out different ones to see which you prefer.

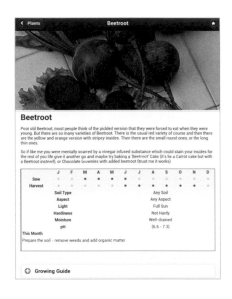

Beginners Gardening Guide

An excellent, extensive guide for anyone new to the delights of gardening. It has categories covering topics such as plant nutrients, garden design, gardening ideas, flower gardens and vegetable gardens. Even for experienced gardeners there will be some useful tips, hints and ideas here too.

BigOven 350,000+ Recipes

An app that does pretty much as it says. There are recipes for all kinds of cooking. You can also get ideas for using up leftovers by entering ingredients and then viewing the suggestions (although this is not always the most accurate).

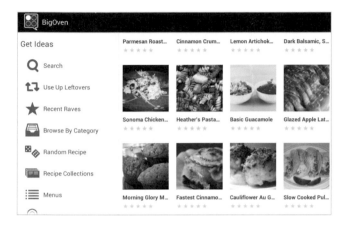

Some of the categories in BigOven come under the Pro heading, which means you have to create an account to view them, which is free to do.

Jamie's 20 Minute Meals

Mouthwatering recipes and cooking tips from TV chef Jamie Oliver. It is a paid-for app and offers numerous quick, healthy and tasty recipes. It also has a section for items for your shopping list for the recipes.

...cont'd

Cocktail Flow – Drink Recipes

For anyone wanting to unravel the mysteries of the cocktail maker, this is the ideal app. Dozens of cocktail recipes, listed by name, base drink, color and type. When a cocktail is selected, its ingredients are listed along with any equipment required to make it, and also preparation instructions.

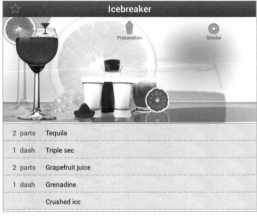

Beware

Try to keep your alcohol consumption within recommended guidelines. There are apps that you can use to keep a record of the amount you drink – see page 95.

WS (Wine Secretary) – Wine and Cellar

Wine is not only a pleasant accompaniment to food, or enjoyable on its own; it can also be an interesting hobby. This app contains details of thousands of types of wine and enables you to build up a list of all of your favorites. There is also a free wine dictionary app that can be downloaded.

How to Draw – Easy Lessons

An excellent app for developing your drawing and painting skills. Once you have selected a drawing, you can move through it step-by-step from the beginning, until it is completed. You can follow the steps on a sheet of paper so that when the tutorial is finished you will have your own version of the picture.

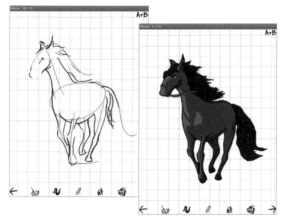

Museums

Some of the best Android apps for museums can locate attractions in individual cities. Enter 'Museums' and the name of a city into the Play Store Search box to see if there is a museum app for that city. The majority cover US cities, and their locations can also be viewed on a city map.

Hot tip

Some museums have live wallpaper apps which can be used as the background on your tablet. Enter the name of a museum, such as the Louvre, to see if there is one with live wallpaper. These tend to be images of the museum itself rather than its contents. See page 36 for how to change the background on your tablet.

Health and Fitness

Keeping fit and healthy should be a fun and varied part of life. In the Play Store there are apps covering areas to ensure that you have a good time keeping in shape.

Simply Yoga

Yoga is an excellent exercise which is beneficial for overall fitness and flexibility. This app has video demonstrations of different techniques, and there is also a spoken commentary that leads you through each one.

Don't forget

For the yoga and workout apps, the videos can be paused by tapping on the button in the middle, at the top of the screen. Tap it again to continue.

Daily Workouts

Similar to the yoga app, this one contains a range of exercises with the same video walk-through format. Exercises can be selected for different parts of the body.

Change4Life Smart Recipes

Healthy eating need not be dull and this app provides a wealth of tasty, healthy recipes, as well as general information about nutrition and eating well.

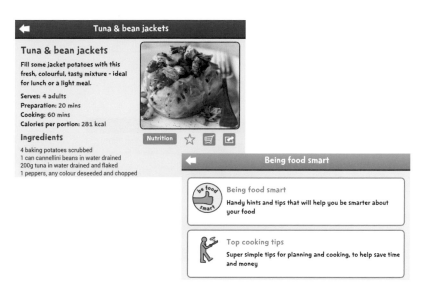

Drink Tracker

Although drinking can be a very enjoyable pastime, it is a good idea to note down how much you are drinking, so that you can keep it within safe limits. This app allows you to compile a record of your daily consumption and has guidelines about safe drinking levels.

If you are using any drinks tracker app, make sure that you fill it in accurately and honestly to ensure that you get a genuine overall picture.

...cont'd

Calorie Counter

There are several calorie counter apps in the Play Store, to help give you an idea of the balance between your calorie intake and the amount of energy that you are using with exercise. They all work in a similar way, in that you have to register with the app, set a target weight and then enter your daily calorie intake and amount of exercise. The app will then keep you up-to-date with whether you are on course to achieve your target weight loss.

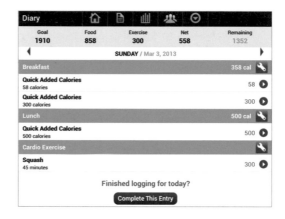

RunKeeper – GPS Track Run Walk

Combined with the GPS on your tablet, this app can be used to log the distance that you have completed during exercise. It can also be used to set up a training plan if you want to undertake a specific type of event, such as a fun run.

Make sure Location services is turned on if you want to use the RunKeeper app. This can be found in **Settings** > **Location** and drag the **Location** button at the top of the window to **On**.

First aid by British Red Cross

An excellent reference for general first aid. Compiled by the world-renowned British Red Cross, it contains videos, diagrams and advice about a range of medical situations. There is also an Emergency button that can be used for specific advice if you are in a life-threatening situation.

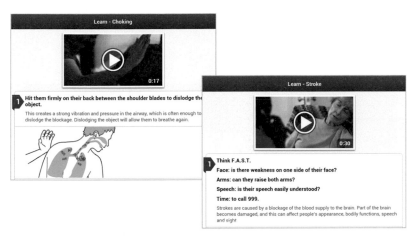

Getting medical advice on the internet or through apps is no substitute for consulting with your own doctor. If you are worried about something, speak to your doctor first.

Nature Sounds Relax and Sleep

Getting a good night's sleep is one of the foundations of good general health. This app provides a range of soothing sounds from nature, such as waterfalls, birdsong and forest sounds, to help you get to sleep. There is also a timer that can be set so that the app turns off after a certain period of time, so that it is not playing all night.

Family History

Researching family history has enjoyed a remarkable growth since it became possible to check up details on the internet. This has now extended to tablet apps, which you can use to create family trees.

Ancestry

This app is linked to the Ancestry website. The app can be used to create your own family tree, but you have to create an account on the relevant Ancestry website for your location in order to be able to search historical records.

Don't forget

Researching family history can be a compelling hobby, and once you start you may find that you want to keep looking further and further into your family background.

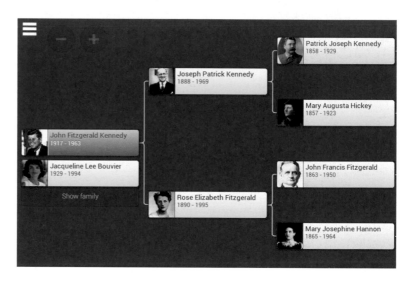

FamilySearch Tree

Similar to the Ancestry app, in that it links to the **FamilySearch.org** website for registered users of this service. People, photos, text and also video can be added to the family trees that are created here.

Family Tree

Not strictly a family history app, this enables you to create a family sharing environment within Facebook, where family members can share information and also access a shared calendar for family events.

6 Tablet Entertainment

Android tablets are not only useful; they are also great fun. This chapter shows how to make the most of your tablet as your own personal entertainment center. It details how to obtain, manage and listen to music, download and watch movies and TV shows, read all of your favorite books and magazines, take photos then view, manage, edit and share your digital images.

100 Using Google Play

101 Music on Android

102 Downloading Music

104 Playing Music

107 Managing Music

108 Pinning Music

110 Movies and TV Shows

114 Obtaining Books

116 Around an Ebook

118 Adding Notes

120 Adding Bookmarks

121 Definitions and Translations

122 Using Cameras

124 Adding Photos

126 Viewing Photos

129 Adding Folders

130 Editing Photos

132 Sharing Photos

Using Google Play

Google Play is the online store for buying, downloading, using and managing a range of entertainment content. It is accessed at the website:

- **play.google.com**

You need to have a Google Account in order to log in to the Google Play website.

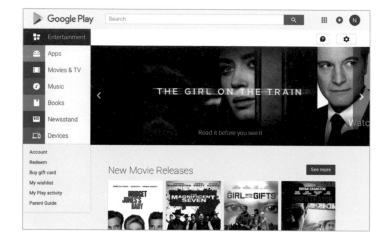

Once you have logged in to Google Play you can download a variety of content:

- Music

- Movies and TV shows

- Apps

- Books

- Newspapers and magazines

Content from Google Play is stored in the cloud so it can then be used on your computer and also your Android tablet. If you delete it from your tablet, either accidentally or on purpose, you can still reinstall it from Google Play. You can also use content downloaded by any of your other Android devices, such as a smartphone.

Don't forget

Content that is downloaded to your Android tablet via the Play Store will also be available on the Google Play website, as long as you are logged in with your Google Account.

Hot tip

If you buy music from either the Play Store or the Google Play website, it can be played on your tablet with streaming (using a Wi-Fi internet connection), or it can be downloaded (pinned) onto your tablet so that you can also listen to it offline (see pages 108-109).

Music on Android

One option for playing music on an Android tablet is the Play Music app. It can be used to play music that has been obtained in a number of different ways:

Play Music

- Downloaded directly to your tablet from the **Play Store**.

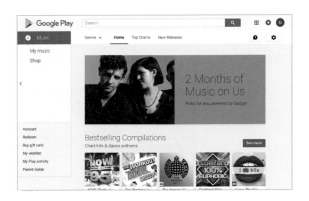

- Bought on **Google Play** and then used on your tablet.

- Uploaded to **Google Play** and then downloaded to your tablet. This can be done with the **Music Manager** that can be installed from Google Play.

- Transferred from your computer directly to your tablet. This is done by connecting your tablet to your computer using the USB cable, and then copying your music to the **Music** folder on your tablet.

- Transferred from another mobile device using Bluetooth.

Google Play Music also offers a subscription service that enables users to download unlimited music through the Play Music app or the Google Play store. There is a 30-day free trial and there are options for either Individual or Family memberships. Google Play Music can be joined when you first open the Play Music app, or from the **Top charts** and **New releases** buttons on the Play Music main menu.

Downloading Music

To use your tablet directly to find and download music from the Play Store:

In some cases, there may be sample content in the Play Music app to help you get started with playing music.

1 Tap on the **Play Music** app to open the music player

Play Music

2 Tap on the **Menu** button to access the Play Music menu, including the **Shop** button

≡   Music library

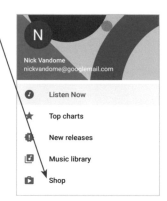

3 Use these buttons to view the relevant sections within the Music section of the Play Store, or

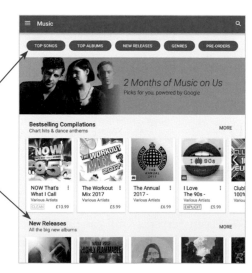

4 Tap on these sections to view the recommended content, or

5 Tap on this button and enter an artist, album or song name into the Search box

6 Locate the item you want to download. For an album, tap on this button to buy the full album, or swipe up the page and tap on the price button next to an individual song

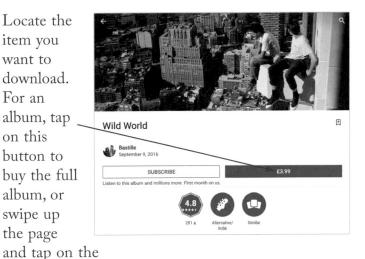

When you buy music from the Play Store it also comes with the related artwork such as album or singles covers.

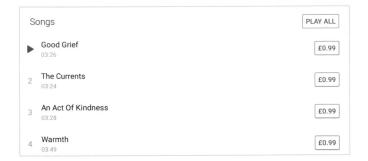

7 Tap on the **Buy** button and enter your Google account password

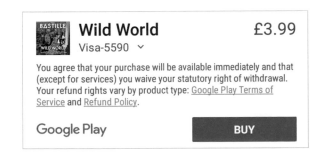

Playing Music

Once you have obtained music on your tablet, by whatever means, you can then start playing it and listening to it. To do this:

1 Tap on the **Play Music** app

2 All of the available music is displayed. This includes music from the Google Play website that is only available for streaming at this point, i.e. it needs a Wi-Fi connection to play it

3 Tap on these buttons to view your music content according to **Playlists**, **Instant Mixes**, **Artists**, **Albums**, **Songs** and **Genres**

4 Tap on an item to view the available songs (for an album) or individual tracks

Don't forget

Streaming is a process where digital content is sent to a device over Wi-Fi when it is needed, in order for it to be played continuously on the device. It does not physically download the content onto the device and it remains on the server from where it was streamed.

5 Tap on a song to play it. The currently-playing song is also displayed at the bottom of the Play Music app

6 Tap on the song or album icon to view the song artwork at full size and view the standard playback controls at the bottom of the window

Invest in a reasonable set of headphones to listen to music on your Android tablet. This will usually result in a higher quality sound than through the built-in speakers.

105

7 When a song is playing, this button appears next to it

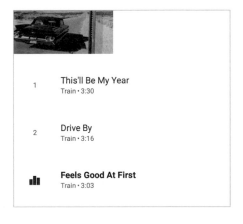

...cont'd

Music controls

When a song is playing there are several options:

1 Use these buttons to, from left to right: go back to the beginning of a song, pause/play a song,  go to the end of a song, i.e. start playing the next one in your music library

Queued songs are those waiting to be played in the Play Music app (see next page).

2 For an album, tap on this button to view the current queue of songs

3 Tap in the middle of the screen to access other controls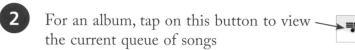

4 Drag this button to move through a song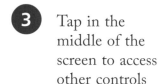

5 Tap on this button to shuffle the songs in your collection

6 Tap on this button to loop the currently-queued songs

7 Tap on these buttons to rate the song on the Google Play website

Managing Music

When you are playing music there is still a certain amount of flexibility in terms of managing what is playing, and being scheduled to play. This is known as the music queue. To use this to manage your music:

1 Tap on this button next to an album or a song

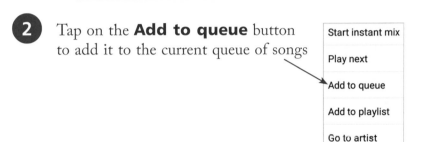

2 Tap on the **Add to queue** button to add it to the current queue of songs

3 View the song queue as shown in Step 2 on the previous page, and tap on this button to hide it

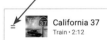

4 When viewing the current queue, tap on the **Menu** button

5 Tap on the **Clear queue** button to remove all of the songs from the current queue

6 When viewing the songs in the queue, tap on the same button as in Step 1 and make one of the related selections, including **Remove from queue**

Hot tip

When viewing the current queue, press and hold on the bar to the left of the song title and drag it to reorder its position in the current queue.

Beware

If you select **Clear queue**, this closes the currently-playing item. However, it does not remove it from your tablet and it remains available in the Play Music app.

Pinning Music

Music that is bought from the Play Store or the Google Play website is available for streaming on your tablet using your Wi-Fi internet connection. This means that the music is sent from the Google servers, where it is stored. This means that it is always backed up and always available.

However, if you are not able to use Wi-Fi you will probably still want to listen to your music, such as when you are traveling. This can be done by pinning the required music to your tablet so that it is physically stored there. To do this:

Items that are not pinned to your device will not be available when you do not have a Wi-Fi connection.

108

1 Access the Play Music Menu and toggle On or Off the **Downloaded only** button to view the music on your tablet that has already

been downloaded to it, rather than just being stored within the Google cloud (i.e. the server that keeps the music that you have bought)

2 For **Downloaded only**, the items that are stored on your tablet are shown

3 The icons denote the status of each item according to whether it is downloaded to the device or not. A grayed-out button indicates an item that has been accessed from the Play Store or Google Play website but has not been downloaded to the device. An orange button with a white tick indicates that an item has been downloaded to your tablet, i.e. pinned

4 Tap on a grayed-out button so that the icon turns orange, to start the process for pinning the item to your tablet

5 The item will be downloaded for storing on your tablet. This is indicated in the Notifications bar by the pin icon

6 Swipe down on the Notifications bar to see the progress of the track(s) being downloaded

> ↓ Google Play Music · now
> The Best Of The Proclaimers - The Proclaimers   16%

7 Tap on an item in Step 6 to view the full download queue

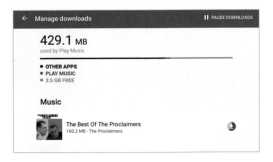

Beware

The more music that you download to your tablet, the more storage space it will take up.

Movies and TV Shows

There are different ways in which video content can be viewed on your Android tablet:

- Downloading movies and TV shows from the Play Store or the Google Play website.

- Transferring (uploading) your own videos to your tablet.

- Watching videos on YouTube.

To obtain movies or TV shows from the Play Store:

Don't forget

Some tablets have their own default movies app, which will be linked to their own app store. If this is the case, the Play Movies app can still be downloaded from the Play Store, and content can be bought from there.

1 Tap on the **Play Movies & TV** app

2 Tap here and tap on the **My library** button to view available content on your tablet. This includes movies and TV shows that you have downloaded, and also recommended titles

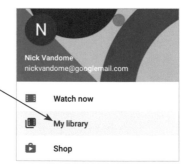

Don't forget

When buying or renting items from the Play Store there are usually options for doing so in Standard Definition (SD) or High Definition (HD).

3 Tap on an item in the **My library** section to view it

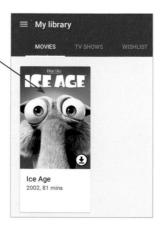

4 Tap on the **Shop** button in Step 2 to view the available movies and TV shows in the Play Store

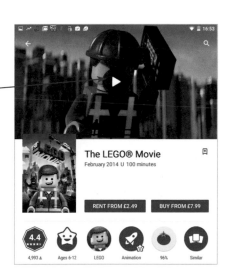

5 The **Movies & TV** section of the Play Store is similar to those for the other types of content

6 Tap on the main panels to view highlighted or recommended movies and TV shows

7 Tap on an item to view details about it. Tap here to watch a preview clip of the item

8 Tap on these buttons to rent or buy a movie or TV show. It will then be made available within the Play Movies app

Tap the **Genres** button at the top of the Movies & TV window to view the different categories. These include Action & Adventure, Animation, Comedy, Documentary, Drama, Family, Horror, Romance, Sci-Fi and Thriller.

The menu options in the Movies section of the Play Store include adding the currently-viewed title to a Wishlist for buying or downloading later, redeeming a voucher, viewing your account details, viewing general Play Store settings, and help options.

...cont'd

9 Tap on the **Rent** (or **Buy**) button to accept the Play Store terms and conditions

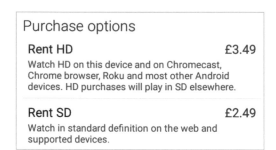

Purchase options

Rent HD	£3.49

Watch HD on this device and on Chromecast, Chrome browser, Roku and most other Android devices. HD purchases will play in SD elsewhere.

Rent SD	£2.49

Watch in standard definition on the web and supported devices.

10 Enter your Google Account password and tap on the **Continue** button to complete the purchase

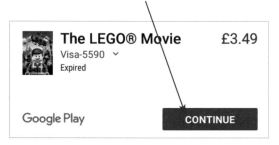

The LEGO® Movie	£3.49
Visa-5590 ⌄	
Expired	

Google Play | CONTINUE

11 Tap on the **Play** button to start playing your purchase. This is done by streaming it from the internet using Wi-Fi. Tap on the **Watch** button to download the item to your tablet so that you can play it at any time, even if you are not connected to the internet

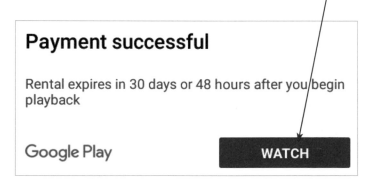

Payment successful

Rental expires in 30 days or 48 hours after you begin playback

Google Play | WATCH

Watching movies and TV shows

When you have bought or rented movies or TV shows you can then watch them on your tablet:

1 Open the **Play Movies & TV** app and view your rented and bought content under the **My Library** section. Tap on the item you want to view

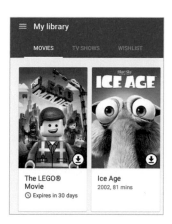

Hot tip

Use an HDMI cable with your tablet so that you can watch movies and TV shows on a High Definition TV.

2 Tap on the **Play** button to start watching a movie or TV show

3 For rented items, you have 48 hours to watch them after you start watching. Tap on the **OK** button to start

4 By default, movies and TV shows are streamed from the Play Store. Tap on the **Download** button to store the content on your tablet so that you can watch it offline

Beware

If you download movies and TV shows to your tablet they can take up a considerable amount of storage space. Rented items will be automatically deleted once the rental period expires.

Obtaining Books

Due to their size and portability, Android tablets are ideal for reading ebooks. There is a wide range that can be downloaded from the Play Store, or from the Google Play website, in a similar way to obtaining music, movies and apps.

The Books section can also be accessed from the main Homepage of the **Play Store** by tapping on the **Menu** button at the top of the screen and tapping on the **Books** button.

Swipe left and right on a panel on the Books Home page to view the items within it.

1 Tap on the **Play Books** app (or access the Google Play website)

Play Books

2 Any books that you already have on your tablet are displayed. Tap on a cover to open a specific title

3 Tap on the **Menu** button and tap on the **Shop** button

4 Books can be browsed for and downloaded in a similar way as for other Play Store content. Tap on these buttons to view books according to these headings

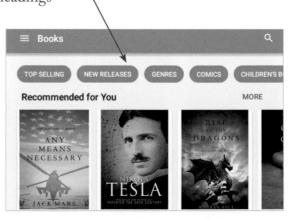

The Kindle app can be downloaded from the Play Store for reading books. If you already have a Kindle account your books will be available through the Kindle app on your tablet.

5 Tap on a title to view details about it

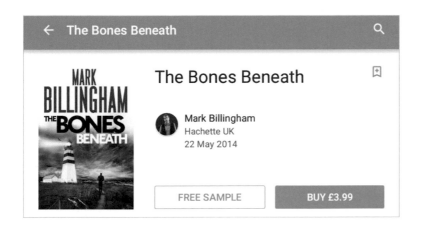

Hot tip

One of the categories in the Play Store Books section is for **Top Free** books. Some classic titles also have free versions if the copyright has expired after a certain period of time following the author's death.

6 When you find a book you want to read, tap on the **Free Sample** button (if there is one) or the **Buy** button (with the price)

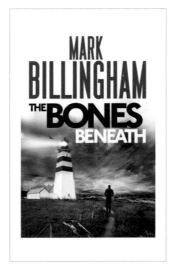

Hot tip

Check out the ebook version of this title and other **In Easy Steps** ebooks in the Play Store. Samples for all titles are downloadable for free:

7 When any book from the Play Books store has been downloaded to your tablet, it is available within your Play Books library

8 Tap in the middle of the page to access the reading controls

Around an Ebook

Once you have downloaded ebooks to your tablet you can start reading them. Due to their format there is a certain amount of electronic functionality that is not available in a hard copy version. To find your way around your ebook:

Don't forget

You can also move to the next or previous page by tapping at the right-hand or left-hand edge of a page.

1 Swipe left and right on a page to move backwards or forwards by one page

2 Tap in the middle of a page to access the reading controls toolbars at the top and bottom of the screen

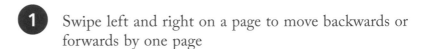

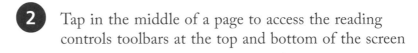

3 Drag this button to move through the book

4 Tap on this button to access the book's table of contents. Tap on a heading to move to that point in the book

Hot tip

To delete an ebook from the Play Books app, tap on this button below the book cover and tap on the **Delete from library** button. The book can be reinstalled from the Play Store if you want to place it in your library again. This is free to do.

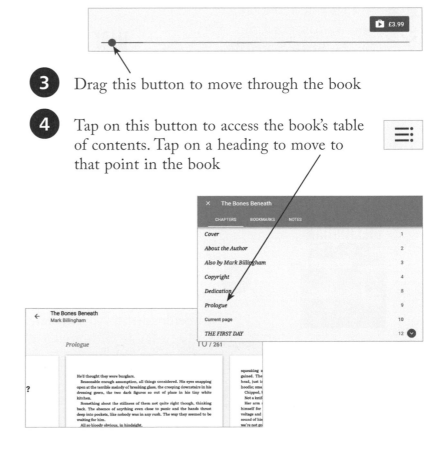

5 Tap on the **Menu** button to access the specific settings for the title you are reading

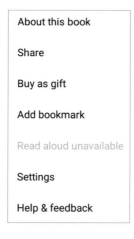

About this book

Share

Buy as gift

Add bookmark

Read aloud unavailable

Settings

Help & feedback

Tap on the **Settings** button in Step 7 to access options for changing the screen brightness for the book being read, and select text and background combinations – black text on a white background, black text on a sepia background or white text on a black background.

6 Tap on this button to select text options   Aa

7 Tap on these buttons to select different font styles

TT   ⚙

A   A   A
Original   Sans   Literata   Me

T   100%   T

‡≡   100%   ↕≡

≡ Default   ▼

8 Tap on the **Font Size** buttons to increase or decrease the font size by one step each time. Tap on the **Line Height** buttons (below the text buttons) to increase or decrease the space between lines

Adding Notes

If you like taking notes while you are reading books, you no longer have to worry about jotting down your thoughts in the margins or on pieces of paper. With Play Books ebooks you can add your own electronic notes and also insert bookmarks at your favorite passages. To do this:

1 Press and hold on a word to activate the two blue text selection markers

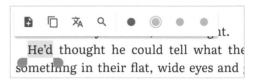

When text is selected, tap on one of the colors on the toolbar to change the color with which it is highlighted.

2 Drag one of the blue markers over the text to select it and access the top toolbar

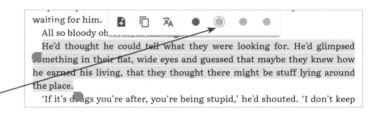

3 Tap on this button to add a note

4 Enter a note for the selected text and tap on the **Save** button on the top toolbar

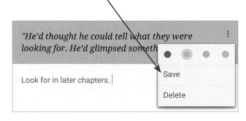

5 A note is indicated by a small yellow icon next to the highlighted text. Tap on this to edit the note

> He'd thought he could tell what they were looking for. He'd glimpsed something in their flat, wide eyes and guessed that maybe they knew how he earned his living, that they thought there might be stuff lying around the place.

6 To view all of your notes, tap on the **Table of Contents** button and tap on the **Notes** tab

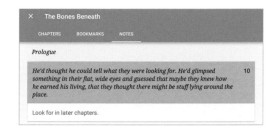

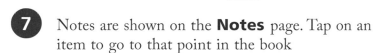

7 Notes are shown on the **Notes** page. Tap on an item to go to that point in the book

8 To delete a note, access it in the book, tap on the yellow note icon and then tap on the **Menu** button

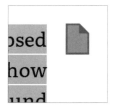

9 On the top toolbar, tap on the **Delete** button

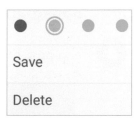

10 Tap on the **Remove** button to confirm the action

Adding Bookmarks

One of the great things about a hard copy book is that you can physically mark pages or insert a bookmark so that you can keep your place. However, with ebooks this functionality has been added so that you can bookmark as many pages as you like, for quick access.

Beware

You can add numerous bookmarks throughout a book. However, if you add too many the **Bookmarks** tab may become cluttered and it will be harder to find items.

1 To bookmark a page in a book, tap in the top right-hand corner. A blue bookmark icon appears. Tap again to remove it

ONE

You want the good news or the bad news?
　　That's what Detective Chief Inspector Russell Brigstocke had said to him back then. Eating his biscuits and trying his patience. Sitting cheerfully on the edge of his bed in that hospital as though they were just old mates chewing the fat. Like Thorne hadn't almost bled to death a few days earlier, like what he laughably called his career wasn't hanging in the balance.
　　Delivering the verdict.
　　Good news. Bad news...

2 Bookmarks can also be added at any time by tapping on the **Menu** button and tapping on the **Add bookmark** button (once a bookmark has been added, this action can be used to remove a bookmark too)

About this book

Share

Buy as gift

Add bookmark

3 Bookmarks are included under the **Table of Contents** button. Tap on the **Bookmarks** tab to view the available bookmarks

4 Tap on a bookmark to go to that location

× The Bones Beneath

CHAPTERS　　BOOKMARKS　　NOTES

THE FIRST DAY

THE FIRST DAYWITH A WORD, WITH A LOOKONEYou want the good news or the bad news? That's what Detect 　　12

ONE

ONEYou want the good news or the bad news? That's what Detective Chief Inspector Russell Brigstock 　　13

Definitions and Translations

Finding definitions

It is always satisfying to learn the meaning of new words, and when reading an ebook on your tablet this can be done at any point in the text:

1 Press and hold on the word for which you want the definition

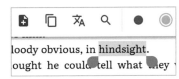

2 The definition appears at the bottom of the screen. Drag the box upwards to view it at the top of the page

hindsight
ˈhʌɪn(d)sʌɪt

noun
1: understanding of a situation or event only after it has happened or developed.

Translations

To see what the text of a book looks like in a different language, use the **Translate** option:

1 Press and hold on a word and drag one of the markers to highlight a piece of text

2 Tap on the **Translate** button

3 Tap on this button to select a language

4 The translation is shown beneath the two selected languages

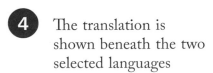

The translation option can be slightly hit-or-miss at times, so don't rely on it for any important translation tasks or projects.

Using Cameras

Most tablets have their own built-in cameras, which can be used to capture photos directly onto the device. The quality of these vary between makes of tablet: some are good quality cameras intended to be used for taking photos in a range of conditions. Others are mainly for use as a webcam for video calls (these are front-facing cameras). To use the camera:

Hot tip

Press once on the screen to focus the current scene.

1 Tap on the **Camera** app

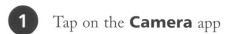
Camera

2 The Camera app displays the current scene, and the control buttons are displayed at the side (landscape view) or at the bottom (portrait view)

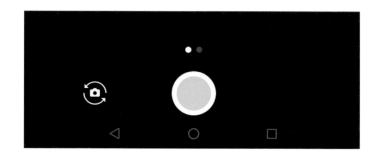

Don't forget

By default, photos captured with the Camera are displayed in the **Photos** app.

3 Tap on this button to take a photo

4 Further controls are available at the top of the screen

5 Tap on this button to switch between the front- and rear-facing cameras

6 Tap on this button to access the self-timer option

7 Tap on this button to toggle on and off a grid over the screen, for composing photos

8 Tap on this button to access the settings for changing white balance

9 Tap on this button to access the settings for how the flash operates

10 Tap on the menu button in the top left-hand corner to access the camera options, including those for **Panorama**, and creating special effects (**Photo Sphere** and **Lens Blur**)

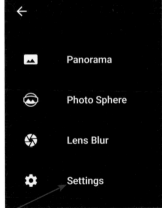

11 When the camera options are displayed, tap on the **Settings** button to access the camera's settings, including those for the resolution and quality of the images that are captured

Hot tip

The options in Step 10 can also be accessed by swiping to the right from the left-hand edge of the screen.

Hot tip

Swipe from right to left on the camera screen to access the mode for capturing video footage.

123

Beware

If you keep a lot of photos on your tablet this will start to take up its storage space.

Hot tip

Personal videos can also be transferred in the same way as with photos. Copy them into the **Videos** folder of your tablet. Videos can also be recorded with the video function in the Camera app (see second tip on page 123).

Adding Photos

Android tablets are great for storing and, more importantly, displaying your photos. The screen size of most tablets is ideal for looking at photos, and you can quickly transform it into your own mobile photo album. In addition, it is also possible to share all of your photos in a variety of ways.

Obtaining photos

You can get photos onto your tablet in a number of ways:

- Transferring photos from your computer directly to your tablet, via a USB cable.

- Transferring photos from your camera to your tablet. This is usually done by inserting your camera's memory card into a card reader connected to your computer, and then transferring your photos.

- Copying photos from an email.

- Downloading from a website or cloud storage facility.

- Transferring photos from another device via Bluetooth.

Once you have captured or transferred photos to your tablet you can then view, edit and share them using the **Photos** app. Photos in the Photos app are stored in different albums, which are created automatically when photos are taken, transferred or downloaded from an email.

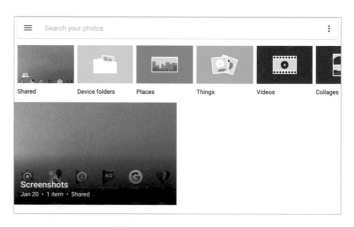

Copying from email

Email is a good method of obtaining photos on your tablet; other people can send their photos to you in this way and you can also email your own photos from a computer, a smartphone or another mobile device. To use photos from email:

1 Open the email containing the photo and tap on this button to download it

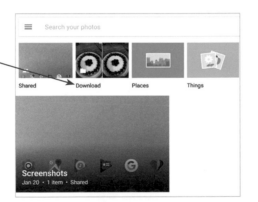

2 The photo will be saved in the **Download** folder within the **Photos** app. This will be created if it is not already there

3 Tap on the photo to open it at full size in the Photos app

Don't forget

Once the **Download** folder has been created, all other photos downloaded from emails will be placed here.

The Photos app has been updated in Android 7.0 Nougat.

The default albums in the Photos app are initially empty.

Viewing Photos

Once you have obtained photos on your Android tablet you can start viewing, managing and editing them.

1 Open the **Photos** app and tap on the **Menu** button at the top of the Photos window to view the options

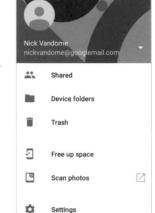

2 Tap on the **Device folders** button from the menu

3 Tap on the **Albums** button at the bottom of the screen to view the available albums

4 Tap on the **Photos** button at the bottom of the screen to view specific photos

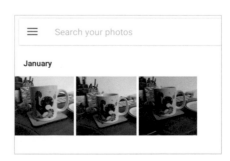

The photos in the Photos app can be worked with and viewed in different ways:

1 Open the **Photos** app and access the **Photos** section as shown on the previous page

Photos

2 The folders and their content are displayed. Tap on a folder to view its contents (if there are more items than appear on the screen)

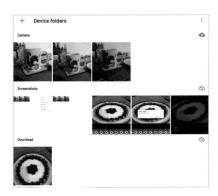

3 In the main window, tap on the **Menu** button and tap on the **Select...** button to select individual photos

4 Use the **Menu** button to view the options for working with the images in the folder. This includes selecting items, changing the layout format on the screen to Day, Month or Year view or creating new items, such as a new album

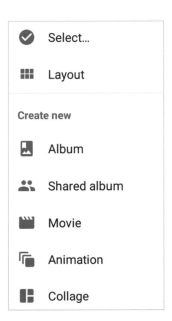

Select...

Layout

Create new

Album

Shared album

Movie

Animation

Collage

The **Layout** of photos can be in Day, Month or Year view.

Don't forget

...cont'd

5 To select items, click on the **Select...** button in Step 4 on the previous page and tap on the items you want to select, denoted by a blue circle with a white tick

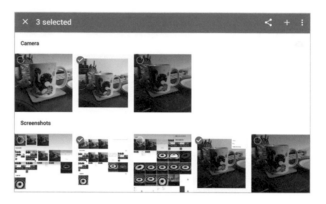

6 Tap on a photo to view it at full size. Tap on this button to access the photo's menu options

7 Select options from the menu, including creating a slideshow, adding the photo to an album, using it as a contact photo or wallpaper image, printing the photo or deleting it from the device

Slideshow

Add to album

Use as

Print

Delete device copy

Adding Folders

In addition to the pre-inserted device folders, new ones can be added either from the Photos or the Albums section of the Photos app. To do this:

1 Tap on the **Menu** button

2 Tap on the **Album** button under the **Create new** heading

3 Tap on the photos to be included in the album and tap on the **Create** button

4 Tap here and give the album a name, and then tap on the tick symbol

5 The new album is included in the Device folders section

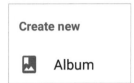

Individual photos can be added to albums by viewing them at full size, tapping on the **Menu** button as in Step 6 on the previous page, tapping on the **Add to album** button, and selecting the required album.

Editing Photos

Although the Photos app is more for viewing photos, it does have a few editing options so that you can tweak and enhance your images. To access and use these:

1 Open an album, select a single photo and select **Edit photo** from the **Menu** button, or

2 Tap on a photo to view it. Tap on this button to access the editing options

Beware

Add small editing changes at a time, otherwise the effect may look too severe.

3 Tap on this button on the bottom toolbar to access the filter options. Tap on one of the filters to apply it to the photo

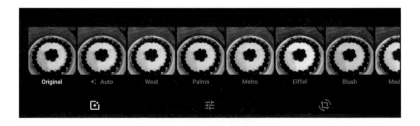

Original   Auto   West   Palma   Metro   Eiffel   Blush   Mod

...cont'd

4 Tap on this button to select a range of color editing functions, including editing the light and color of the photo. Drag the sliders to change the effect

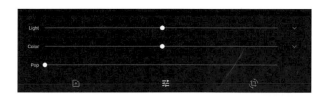

5 Tap on this button next to one of the color editing options to access sliders for editing elements within the main category

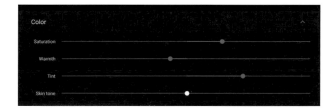

6 To crop a photo, tap on the **Crop** button and drag the resizing handles as required

7 Tap on this button to **Rotate** the photo manually or left or right

8 Tap on the **Save** button to save any editing changes that have been made

SAVE

Hot tip

Most photos benefit from some cropping, to give the main subject more prominence.

Sharing Photos

It can be great fun and very rewarding to share photos with friends and family. With an Android tablet this can be done in several ways:

Don't forget

Social networking sites such as Facebook and Twitter are ideal for sharing photos. Their respective apps can be downloaded from the Play Store, in which case they will also appear as one of the sharing options in Step 2.

1 Select an album or open an individual photo and tap on this button on the top toolbar

2 Select one of the sharing options. This will be dependent on the apps on your tablet

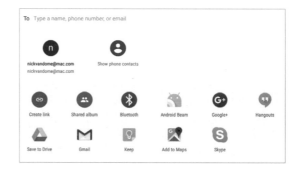

Sharing with Bluetooth
To share with another device with Bluetooth:

Beware

If you are sending photos by Bluetooth, the other device must be paired with your tablet, have Bluetooth turned on, and accept the request to download the photos when they are sent.

1 Access a photo and tap on the **Bluetooth** button option in Step 2 above

2 If your Bluetooth is not on, tap on the **Turn on** button to activate it

3 Select the device with which you want to share your photo(s). These will be sent wirelessly via Bluetooth

7 Keeping in Touch

This chapter shows how to make the most of different email options, social networking sites, your address book and calendars to keep in touch with people.

134 Email on Android

135 Adding Email Accounts

137 Using Email

139 Email Settings

140 Social Networking

142 Keeping an Address Book

144 Using Your Calendar

146 Using Your Google Account

Email on Android

Email is now a standard feature in most people's digital world. Android tablets provide access to any email accounts that you have. With Android 7.0 and higher, the Gmail app is now used for all email services:

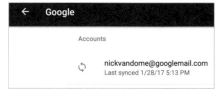

- **Gmail app**. This is the online webmail account provided by Google. When you create a Google Account you will also be provided with a Gmail account. This can be accessed directly from your Android tablet by tapping on the **Gmail** app. It can also be used to link to any of your other email accounts.

Details of email accounts can be viewed within the Accounts section of the Settings app, where new accounts can also be added (which will then be available through the Gmail app).

Don't forget

When you view details of email accounts you can also access the sync settings for each one, by tapping on the account name.

1 Within the Accounts section, tap on the account name

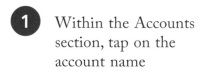

2 The account details are displayed. Tap here to sync the account with the online services for the account, such as for a Google Account

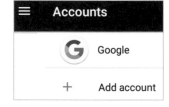

Don't forget

By syncing details with your Google Account this ensures that the information from your tablet is copied to your Google Account, so that both versions are the same.

3 Tap on the **Add account** button in Step 1 and select one of the options, including for adding a new email account

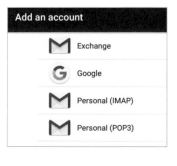

Adding Email Accounts

Email accounts can be added from the **Accounts** section of the **Settings** app, with the **Add account** button as shown on the previous page. In addition, they can also be added directly from the Gmail app. To do this:

1   Tap on the **Gmail** app

2   Select the type of email account that you want to create

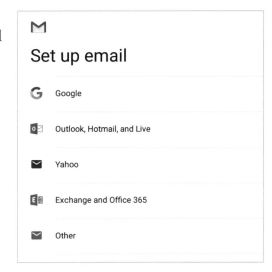

Numerous email accounts can be added to the Gmail app and all of them can be accessed from this single app.

3   Enter your email address and tap on the **Next** button. If the account is not recognized automatically, tap on the **Manual Setup** button

...cont'd

4 For a manual setup, enter the details for the incoming and outgoing email servers. These can be obtained from your email provider. Tap on the **Next** button after each step

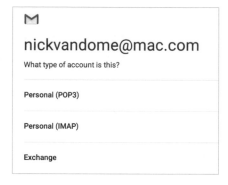

The **Account options** in Step 5 include specifying a notification for when email arrives; syncing email on the server; and automatically downloading email attachments over Wi-Fi.

5 After the server settings, select the **Account options** you want to use and tap on the **Next** button

NEXT

6 The setup is confirmed. Tap on the **Next** button to open the **Gmail** app and view your messages

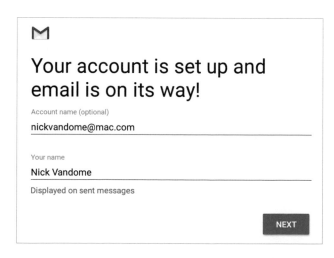

Using Email

Viewing emails

Once you have added email accounts you can view them using the Gmail app.

1 Tap on the **Gmail** app
Gmail

2 Tap here to view the available accounts. Tap on an account to view the messages in it

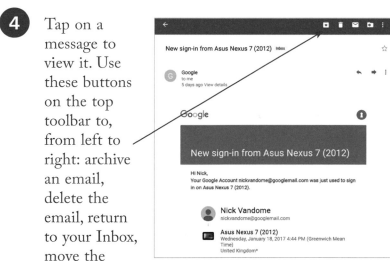

3 Tap on the **Inbox** button to view the messages in here

4 Tap on a message to view it. Use these buttons on the top toolbar to, from left to right: archive an email, delete the email, return to your Inbox, move the email to another folder and access the email's Menu settings

Don't forget

The most recently read message is displayed with a blue bar next to them on the left-hand side.

...cont'd

Sending an email

To send an email from the **Gmail** app:

1 Tap on the **Compose** button to create a new message

2 A new blank email is created

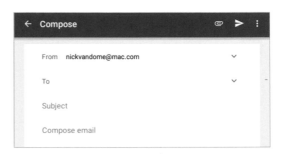

3 Enter a recipient (if the recipient is in your Contacts app, their name will be suggested as you type it), a subject and the body text of the email

4 Tap on the **Send** button on the top toolbar to send the message, or

5 Tap on the **Menu** button and tap on the **Save draft** button to keep it and send it at a later date

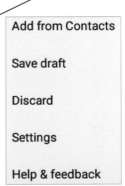

Add from Contacts

Save draft

Discard

Settings

Help & feedback

Email Settings

There are a number of settings that can be applied when using the Gmail app. They can be accessed from the email Inbox or when an individual email is being composed.

1 In either the **Inbox** or an individual email, tap on the **Menu** button

2 Tap on the **Settings** button

3 Tap on an email account to view its settings

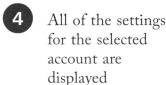

4 All of the settings for the selected account are displayed

New email accounts can also be added from the main **Settings** screen in Step 3. Tap on the **Add account** button to do this and follow the requested steps.

5 Check on the **Notifications** checkbox to enable email notifications to appear in the Notifications area

6 Tap on the **Signature** button to add a message that automatically appears at the end of your emails

Social Networking

Social networking has transformed the way in which we communicate. There are now numerous websites and apps with which we can share information, photos, thoughts, opinions, jokes and almost anything else. Facebook and Twitter have been two of the main players in this area, but there is also a range of other sites in the social networking sphere, offering differing options for staying in touch.

On a tablet, the range of social networking sites can be accessed through a web browser or by using the dedicated apps that can be downloaded from the **Play Store**, from within the **Social** category. It is generally better to use the app for a specific social networking site, as the interface is more suited to the tablet.

Tap on a social networking app to see details about it, and tap on the **Install** button to download it to your tablet.

Some of the most popular social networking sites are:

Facebook

Despite the range of new sites this is still one of the most widely-used social networking tools. To use Facebook you have to first register, which is free. You can then link up with your friends, and share a variety of content, by searching for them and inviting them with a Friend Request.

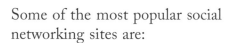

Twitter

Twitter is a microblogging site where users post short messages of up to 140 characters. Once you have joined Twitter, which is free, you can follow other users to see what they are saying, and have people follow you too. Messages on Twitter are known as "tweets".

140

Don't forget

Google+ is a social networking app that is similar to Facebook in terms of creating online communities for sharing content. It is a built-in app on Google tablets, and can be accessed from the All Apps area.

G+
Google+

Snapchat

Snapchat has quickly caught the imagination of social networking users. It is a messaging service that allows users to send photos and videos to their Snapchat friends, or groups of people. Once these are accessed, they remain visible for up to 10 seconds and then they are deleted. Text and graphics can be added to items when they are sent, and one of the most frequent uses is for sending self-portraits (selfies). There is the potential for inappropriate material to be sent, and saved, so be careful what you include.

Pinterest

This is an online pinboard, where you can bookmark and "pin" items of interest and upload your own content for other people to pin. Registration is required for the site, which is free. You can have several of your own pinboards and organize them by subjects, and share them with other Pinterest users. You can also add content to your pinboards from websites with the Pinterest button.

Instagram

This is a popular photo and video sharing site. Followers can be added by users and they can then comment and "like" photos. By default, the security settings are for public viewing of content, so these should be changed if you only want your own followers to be able to view your content.

Tumblr

This combines the functions of a number of other sites and can be used like an online diary, where you post your photos, videos and own thoughts and ideas in a series of blogs. These posts can be viewed by your Tumblr contacts, or everyone if the account is public. If you have Facebook and Twitter accounts, your Tumblr content can also be linked to these. It can be harder to make your account private on Tumblr than on some other sites.

Don't forget

YouTube is one of the great successes of the internet age. It is a video sharing site, with millions of video clips covering every subject imaginable. There is a built-in YouTube app on most Android tablets, which can be accessed from the All Apps button.

YouTube

Keeping an Address Book

An important part of staying in touch with people is having an up-to-date address book. On an Android tablet this can be done with the **Contacts** app:

Some tablets have their own default address book and calendar apps, which can be used in a similar way to the ones shown on the following pages. The Contacts app and the Calendar app can be downloaded from the Play Store, and these are the best ones to use if you want to sync your items with your Google Account.

1 Tap on the **Contacts** app

2 Tap on this button to create a new contact

3 Tap in the fields to enter the contact's details

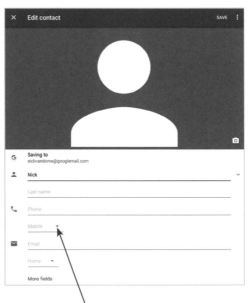

142

Once contact information such as email address and phone number has been added, these items will appear when you start to enter the contact's name in a relevant app, e.g. Gmail for sending an email. You can also start an email or a Skype call (see page 164) by tapping on a contact's email address or phone number in the Contacts app.

4 Tap here on one of the items to view additional options

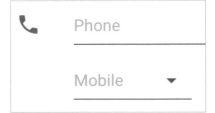

5 Select one of the sub-categories from the main category selected in the previous step

6 Each new contact is added to the Homepage of the Contacts app. Tap on a contact to view their details

Entries in the Contacts app are also available online in your Google Account. This means that you can access them whenever you are online on another computer too.

143

7 Tap on the **Edit** button on the top toolbar to edit the contact's details, in the same way as for adding them when the contact was first created

8 Tap on the **Menu** button on the top toolbar to view the menu options for the selected contact, including linking it to your own account, deleting it, sharing it with other people or creating a shortcut to it on the Home screen

Using Your Calendar

The Calendar app can be used to add items such as events, meetings and birthdays. You can use these on your tablet, and they will also be available online from any internet-enabled computer or mobile device via your Google Account. To use the Calendar:

Don't forget

A range of national and public holidays are pre-inserted into your calendar, usually based on your location.

144

1 Tap on the **Calendar** app

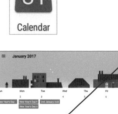
Calendar

2 The calendar is displayed, and the view can be customized in a number of ways

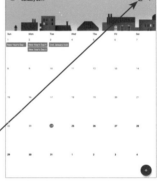

3 Tap on this button to view the current day at any point

24

4 Tap on the **Menu** button at the top of the window to view the calendar by day, week or month, or to display all of the events that have been added (Schedule)

☰	Schedule
☰	Day
▥	Week
▦	Month
🔍	Search

☰

5 Swipe left and right on the main calendar to view different days, weeks and months. Tap on a day to go to that point

Adding events

One of the main uses for the calendar is adding events:

1 In any view, tap and hold on a day or a time slot and tap on the **Tap to create** option, or

The Calendar is linked to your Google Account, and events will be displayed here if you access your Calendar at accounts.google.com

2 In any view, tap on this button to add a new event

3 Tap on the **Event** button

If the full range of options are not visible in the Event window, tap on the **More options** button.

More options

4 Enter the details for the event including: what, where, from, to and a description

5 Tap here to select a recurring event and specify the frequency

6 Tap here to select a time for a reminder for the event. Reminders appear as notifications on the Lock screen, or in the Notifications area

Recurring events can be used for items such as birthdays.

7 Tap on the **Save** button to add the event

Using Your Google Account

When you have a Google Account, the information that you enter into your communication apps such as Gmail, Calendar and Contacts can also be viewed online whenever you are logged in to your account. To do this:

1 Tap on your Google Account details under **Settings > Accounts**

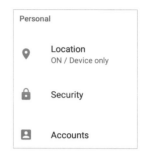

2 Drag the buttons to **On** for each item that you want to sync with your online Google Account

3 Log in to your Google Account online at **accounts.google.com**
Tap on one of the relevant services to view the information from your Android app that has been synced with your Google Account, such as the Calendar. The details should be the same as for the item on your tablet

⑧ Browsing the Web

This chapter looks at browser options on Android, and also using all of your favorite websites with the default Chrome browser.

148 Android Web Browsers

149 Opening Pages

150 Bookmarking Pages

152 Links and Images

153 Using Tabs

154 Being Incognito

155 Browser Settings

Android Web Browsers

Web browsing is an essential part of our digital world, and on Android tablets this functionality is provided by a variety of web browsers customized for this purpose. They can usually display websites in two ways:

- Optimized for viewing on mobile devices, which are versions that are designed specifically for viewing in this format.

- Full versions of websites, rather than the mobile versions, which are the same as used on a desktop computer.

Different Android tablets have different default browsers, but they all have the same general functionality:

- Viewing web pages.

- Bookmarking pages.

- Tabbed browsing, i.e. using tabs to view more than one web page within the same browser window.

If you do not want to use the default browser that is provided with your tablet, there is a range of browsers that can be downloaded, for free, from the Play Store.

Enter **browsers for android** into the **Play Store Search box** to view the available options.

Mobile versions of websites usually have **m.** before the rest of the website address, e.g. **m.mysite.com**

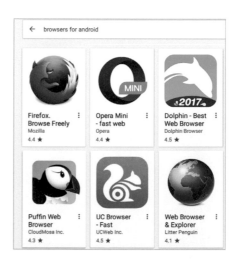

Opening Pages

Web pages can be opened on a tablet in an almost identical way as on a desktop computer or laptop. For some Android web browsers, there is a list of top sites when you open a browser or create a new tab. (The examples on the following pages are for the **Chrome** browser, but other browsers operate in a similar way.)

Don't forget

The Chrome browser can be downloaded from the Play Store if it is not already on your tablet. This is a Google product and integrates closely with other Google apps on your tablet.

1. When you first open Chrome, the **Search/ Address** box at the top of the page can be used to search for keywords or phrases, or you can use it to find specific web pages and sites. Enter text into the **Search/ Address** box

2. Tap on an item with this icon to search for the item over the web. Tap on one to go to a list of results or tap on one to go to that website

3. Tap on an item with this icon to go a web page with the search results for the item

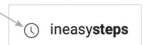

Hot tip

Swipe outwards with your thumb and forefinger on a web page to zoom in on it; pinch inwards to zoom back out. Double-tap with one finger to zoom in and out too, but this zooms in to a lesser degree than swiping.

Bookmarking Pages

The favorite pages that you visit can be bookmarked so that you can find them quickly. To do this:

1 Open the page that you want to bookmark and tap on the star button in the **Search/Address** box

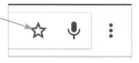

Hot tip

If bookmarks are saved into the **Mobile bookmarks** folder they will also be available on other mobile devices.

2 Tap on the **Edit** button to edit the bookmark

3 Tap in the **Folder** box to specify a folder into which you want to save the bookmark

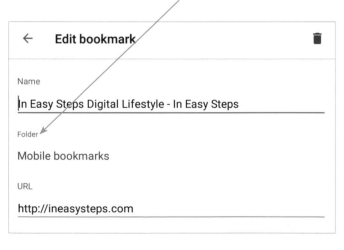

← **Edit bookmark** 🗑

Name

In Easy Steps Digital Lifestyle - In Easy Steps

Folder

Mobile bookmarks

URL

http://ineasysteps.com

4 Tap on a folder to select it, or tap on the **New folder** button to create a new folder to use

←	**Choose folder**	
+	New folder...	
📁	Mobile bookmarks	✓

5 Give the folder a name and tap on the tick symbol to create the folder

←	**Add folder**	✓

Nature

Parent folder
Mobile bookmarks

6 When a page has been bookmarked, the star button turns blue

Viewing bookmarks
To view pages that have been bookmarked:

1 To view bookmarks, tap on the **Menu** button and tap on the **Bookmarks** button

New tab

New incognito tab

Bookmarks

⋮

The **Menu** button can also be used to open a new tab. See page 153 for more details.

2 The bookmarked pages are displayed in their relevant folders. Tap on one to open that page

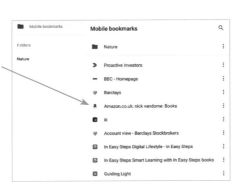

Links and Images

Links and images are both essential items on websites; links provide the functionality for moving between pages and sites, while images provide the all-important graphical element. To work with these:

1   Tap and hold on a link to access its menu (tap once on a link to go directly to the linked page). The options on the menu are for

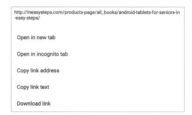

opening the link in a new tab, opening it in a new tab that does not get recorded by the browser's history (**Open in incognito tab**), copying the web address or link text so that it can be shared with someone or pasted into a document, and downloading the link so that it can be viewed offline

2   Tap and hold on an image to access its menu. The options are for downloading it, viewing it on its own (**Open image in new tab**), searching Google for the image, or sharing it. For the **Open image in new tab** option, the image is displayed on its own on a page

Using Tabs

Tabs are now a common feature on web browsers, and are a function whereby you can open numerous pages within the same browser window. To do this:

1 Tap on this button at the top right-hand corner of the browser window to add a new tab, or

2 Tap on the **Menu** button and tap on the **New tab** button

3 Open a new page from the **Bookmarks** folder or by entering a web address or search word into the **Search/Address** box

4 New tabs are opened at the top of the browser. Tap on the tab heading to move to that page

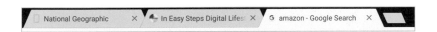

5 If too many tabs are opened for the available space on the screen, they are stacked on top of each other

6 Tap on the cross on a tab to close it

153

Hot tip

If there are a lot of tabs open, swipe left and right on the tabs bar to move between them all.

Being Incognito

If you do not want a record to be kept of the web pages that you have visited, most browsers have a function where you can view pages "in private" so that the details are not stored by the browser. In Chrome, this is performed with the incognito function:

1 Tap on the **Menu** button and tap on the **New incognito tab** button

New tab

New incognito tab

2 The incognito page opens in a new tab, but any other open tabs are not visible (unless they are incognito too). Open a web page in the same way as for a standard tab

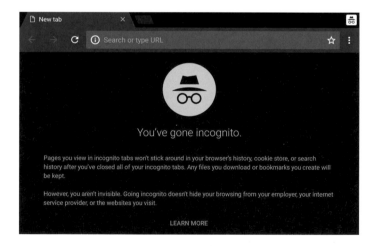

You've gone incognito.

Pages you view in incognito tabs won't stick around in your browser's history, cookie store, or search history after you've closed all of your incognito tabs. Any files you download or bookmarks you create will be kept.

However, you aren't invisible. Going incognito doesn't hide your browsing from your employer, your internet service provider, or the websites you visit.

LEARN MORE

3 Incognito pages are denoted by this icon at the top right-hand corner of the browser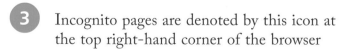

4 Tap on this button to toggle between incognito tabs and standard tabs. In each view, the tabs in the other view are not visible

Browser Settings

Mobile browsers have the usual range of settings that can be accessed from the **Menu** button.

① Tap on the **Menu** button and tap on the **Settings** button

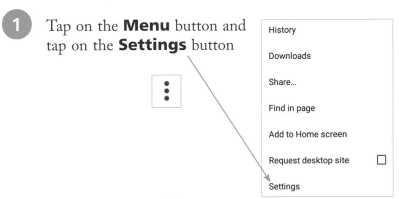

History
Downloads
Share…
Find in page
Add to Home screen
Request desktop site ☐
Settings

Some of the Settings include:

- **Search engine**. This can be used to set a default search engine for the browser.

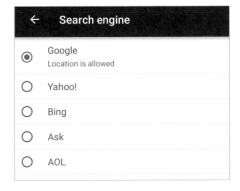

← Search engine
⦿ Google — Location is allowed
○ Yahoo!
○ Bing
○ Ask
○ AOL

- **Auto-fill forms**. Use this to make selections for how online forms are dealt with by the browser.

← Autofill forms ❓
On 🔘
Addresses +
2 Young Street, PH2 0EF
Credit cards +
Visa ·· ▮▮▮ Google Payments

Beware

If other people are going to be using your account on your tablet do not turn on auto-fill options for credit or debit cards. If other people are using the tablet, it is best to set up individual accounts for them – see pages 172-173 for details.

155

...cont'd

- Under the **Advanced** heading, tap on the **Privacy** button to specify how your browsing data is used.

- Under the **Advanced** heading, tap on the **Accessibility** button to specify the text size for viewing web pages.

- Under the **Advanced** heading, tap on the **Site settings** button. Check on or off the options for cookies, JavaScript (which is required to give you full functionality of most websites) and pop-up menus. Tap on the **Location** button to specify whether Google apps can use your current location, and the **All sites** button to view settings for individual websites.

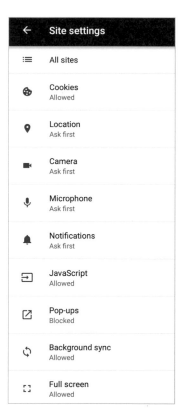

- Under the **Advanced** heading, tap on the **Data Saver** button to specify how web pages are pre-loaded.

A cookie is a small piece of data that is stored by the browser containing information about websites that have been visited.

Pop-ups are unsolicited messages that appear in small windows on a website. They are a form of advertising, and it is usually better to ensure that they do not appear.

9 On Your Travels

Tablets are ideal traveling companions, and this chapter looks at some of the issues connected with this.

158 Traveling with Your Tablet

160 Keeping Your Tablet Safe

161 Airport Security

162 Finding Hotels and Flights

164 Calling with Skype

166 Useful Travel Apps

Traveling with Your Tablet

When you go traveling there are a few essentials that you have to consider: passport, money and insurance, to name three. To this you can add your tablet; it is a perfect traveling companion that can help you plan your trip and keep you informed and entertained when you are away from home.

Uses for traveling

There are a lot of Play Store apps that can be used for different aspects of traveling. However, the built-in apps can also be put to good use before and during your travels:

Hot tip

Social networking sites can be a great asset when you are traveling: you can keep in touch with family and friends, and post your photos and videos as soon as you have taken them so that people can see them even before you get home.

- **Maps**. Use this for accessing maps of your destinations, finding directions and viewing images of areas to which you are traveling.

- **Contacts**. Keep your Contacts app address book up-to-date so that you can use it to send postcards to friends and family and access contact details.

- **Gmail**. With a Wi-Fi connection on holiday you can keep in touch with everyone through the Gmail app and also send them photos of your trip.

- **Play Music**. Use this app to play your favorite music while you are traveling or relaxing at your destination.

- **Photos**. Store photos of your trip with this app and play them back as a slideshow when you get home.

- **Calculator**. Use this to work out the cost of items by converting prices from the local currency. Use it in conjunction with a currency converter for best results.

- **Play Books** (and **Play Newsstand**). Instead of dragging lots of heavy books around, use this app for your holiday library.

Using Google Feeds on your travels

As shown on pages 52-56, Google Feeds can be used to display cards with a range of real-time information. When you are traveling this can be an excellent way to keep informed about your location. The Google Feeds cards can be set to be location specific, so that you can get information about a range of items when you are traveling, including:

- **Weather**. This can be used to get local weather forecasts for your location.

- **Transport**. This can be used to get transport information covering buses and trains, and also road conditions in terms of delays or roadworks.

- **Places**. This can be used to show places of interest for your current location.

For the Google Feeds cards used when traveling, a Wi-Fi or 3G/4G connection is required so that you can connect to the internet to get the relevant information.

To ensure that you get the correct Google Feeds when you are traveling, it has to be set up to access this facility:

1 Tap on the **Google** app

2 Tap on the **Menu** button and tap on the **Settings** button

Tap on the **Customize** button in Step 2 to select the items that you want to appear in your Google Feeds.

3 Select **Accounts & privacy** > **Google activity controls** > **Web & App Activity** and drag the **Web & App Activity** button to **On**

Keeping Your Tablet Safe

By most measures, tablets are valuable items. However, in a lot of countries around the world their relative value can be a lot more than it is to their owners; in some countries the value of a tablet could easily equate to several months' wages. Even in countries where their relative value is not so high they can still be seen as a lucrative opportunity for thieves. Therefore, it is important to try to keep your tablet as safe as possible when you are on vacation. Some points to consider in relation to this are:

- If possible, try to keep your tablet with you at all times, i.e. transport it in a piece of luggage that you can carry rather than having to put it into a large case.

- Never hand over your tablet, or any other of your belongings, to anyone who promises to look after them.

- If you do have to detach yourself from your tablet, try to put it somewhere secure, such as a hotel safe.

- When you are traveling, try to keep your tablet as unobtrusive as possible. This is where a small backpack can prove useful, as it is not immediately apparent that you are carrying a tablet.

- Do not use your tablet in areas where you think it may attract undue interest from the locals, particularly in obviously poor areas. For instance, if you are in a local café the appearance of a tablet may create unwanted attention for you. If in doubt, wait until you get back to your hotel.

- If you are accosted by criminals who demand your tablet then hand it over. No piece of equipment is worth suffering physical injury for.

- Make sure your tablet is covered by your vacation insurance. If not, get separate insurance for it.

- Trust your instincts with your tablet. If something doesn't feel right, then don't do it.

Hot tip

Before you leave for your vacation, make sure that your tablet is backed up. The tablet's contents will be backed up automatically if you have a Google Account. Items to be backed up can be specified in **Settings > Account > Google**. To do a manual backup, use the **Backup & reset** option in the **Personal** section of the **Settings** app. Drag the **Back up my data** button **On**.

Airport Security

Because of the increased global security following terrorist attacks throughout the beginning of the 21st century, the levels of airport security have been greatly increased around the world. This has implications for all travelers, and if you are traveling with a tablet this may add to the security scrutiny which you will face. When dealing with airport security when traveling with a tablet, there are some issues that you should always keep in mind:

- Keep your tablet with you at all times. Unguarded baggage at airports immediately raises suspicion and it can make life very easy for thieves.

- Carry your tablet in a small bag so that you can take it on board as hand luggage. On no account should it be put into your luggage that goes in the hold.

- X-ray machines at airports will not harm your tablet. However, if anyone tries to scan it with a metal detector, ask them if they can inspect it by hand instead.

- Keep a careful eye on your tablet when it goes through the X-ray conveyor belt and try to be there at the other side as soon as it emerges. In some countries there have been stories of people causing a commotion at the security gate just after someone has placed electronic devices on the conveyor belt. While everyone's attention (including yours) is distracted, an accomplice takes the device from the conveyor belt. If you are worried about this you can ask for the security guard to hand-check your tablet rather than putting it on the conveyor belt.

- Make sure the battery of your tablet is fully charged. This is because you may be asked to turn on your tablet to verify that it is just that, and not some other device disguised as a tablet.

- When you are on the plane, keep the tablet in the storage area under your seat, rather than in the overhead locker, so that you know where it is at all times.

Beware

If you put your tablet in your main luggage there is a chance that it could be taken out of it when it is being loaded onto the plane.

Finding Hotels and Flights

The Play Store is an excellent vehicle for finding good value hotel rooms and flights around the world. When hotels have spare capacity, this can quickly be relayed to associated websites, where users can usually benefit from cheap prices and special offers. There are plenty of apps that have details of thousands of hotels around the world, such as:

TripAdvisor

One of the top travel apps, this not only has hotel information but also restaurants, activities and flights. Enter a destination in the Search box and then navigate through the available options.

Hotels.com

A stylish app that enables you to enter search keywords or find local hotels depending on your current location. You can also view any reservations that you have made.

Hot tip

If you are booking hotel rooms, look at several apps as some of them have the same rooms, but at different prices from each other.

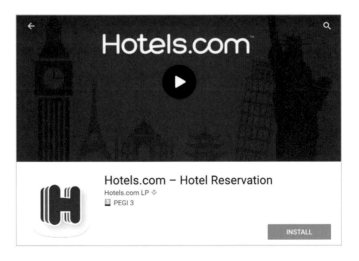

Booking.com

Another good, fully featured hotel app that provides a comprehensive service and excellent prices.

LateRooms.com

An app that specializes in getting the best prices by dealing with rooms that are available at short notice. Some genuine bargains can be found here, for hotels of all categories.

Trivago

Another app for finding good value hotel rooms around the world. Hotels can be viewed according to location and then filtered according to popularity, rating, price, number of stars, and distance from your location.

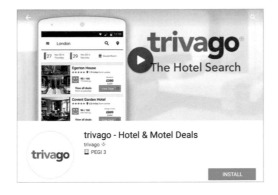

Orbitz

A comprehensive travel app that covers flights, hotels and car rentals. It can also be used to enter details about your itinerary, although you need to create an account and sign in for this.

Kayak

Another all-round travel app that enables you to book flights, hotels and cars. You can also view your itinerary, and there is a flight tracker function too.

Expedia Hotels, Flights & Cars

The mobile app for the popular online travel company, where you can book all of your travel requirements by entering your destination and dates of travel.

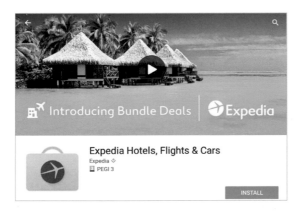

Calling with Skype

Just because you are on vacation does not mean that you cannot keep in touch with family and friends at home, and calls with the Skype app via your tablet are an ideal way to do this. As long as you have Wi-Fi access to the internet, you can make voice and video calls to other Skype users free of charge. To use Skype:

Skype voice and video calls are free to other Skype users. Calls to non-Skype users have to be paid for.

1 Access the **Play Store** and download the Skype app

2 Open **Skype** by tapping on this button

3 If you already have a Skype account, enter your details, or tap on the **Create account** button to create a new account

4 Once signed in, your contacts are displayed under **People** on the Homepage

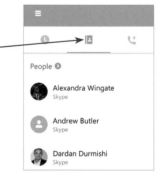

5 Tap on a contact to view their details and contact them by voice or video with these buttons at the top of the window, or by instant messaging with the text box at the bottom of the window

Adding Skype contacts

To add new contacts to call in Skype:

1 Tap here to add new contacts

2 Tap this button to search for new contacts to add

3 Enter a name into the Search box and tap on one of the results

4 Matches for the requested person are shown. Tap on a person's name and tap on the **Add to contacts** button to send a contact request

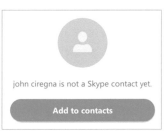

5 The selected person will then be sent a Skype request and they have to accept it before they become a full contact. Enter the text you want to use for the request, or use the default text that is pre-inserted

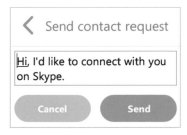

6 Tap on the **Send** button to send the message and request that the person accepts you as a contact

Once you add the Skype app to your tablet, your Skype contacts will also be available in your **Contacts** app.

Calls can also be made directly to numbers, using the keypad. Tap on this button on the main toolbar to access the Skype keypad.

Useful Travel Apps

In addition to hotel and flight apps there are also numerous apps from the Play Store that can be used for several areas of planning and organizing your trip. Some to look at are:

City guides and maps

Enter the name of a major city around the world (New York, London, Paris, Sydney etc.) into the Play Store Search box and you will be presented with a list of results for city guides, maps and transit details for the selected city.

If you visit somewhere recommended in an app such as TripAdvisor, post a review to help give other people more information about it.

TripAdvisor city guides

As above, these are some of the most comprehensive city guides in the Play Store. They include a wide range of information, from restaurants, hotels, attractions, transport and tours, to nightlife and shopping. It also includes reviews and comments from people who have visited the restaurants and sights listed in the app.

Wi-Fi Finder

Using Wi-Fi for accessing the internet and the range of Google services on your tablet is an essential function when using your device at home, and it is just as important when you are away from home. This app locates Wi-Fi access points and hotspots around your current location, and there is also an offline database that lists Wi-Fi hotspots around the world. Tap on the **Wi-Fi Scanner** button to find all Wi-Fi points near you, and tap on the **Public Wi-Fi Near Me** button to view all of the public Wi-Fi points nearby.

If you are traveling somewhere, look up the Wi-Fi hotspots before you leave, as you will not be able to use the app if you are not already connected to Wi-Fi, although you can still use the offline database if you have downloaded it.

167

World Atlas

A basic atlas that can help you plan your trip and find countries around the world. Swipe to move around the globe and pinch outwards with thumb and forefinger to zoom in on an area. Pinch inwards to zoom back out again.

...cont'd

Hot tip

Look up the UNESCO World Heritage website at **whc.unesco.org** for detailed information about these fascinating and diverse areas.

My World Heritage Passport

The UNESCO World Heritage sites offer some of the most stunning and interesting locations around the world. This app enables you to view them by a variety of criteria, and also view a range of information about each site.

XE Currency

This app delivers information about exchange rates for all major world currencies, and also a wealth of background information such as high and low rates and historical charts.

10 Sharing with the Family

This chapter shows how best to give safe access to other family members and guest users.

170 About Multiple Users

172 Adding Family Members

174 Switching Between Users

175 Guest Users

176 Restricted Profiles

About Multiple Users

Because of the power and flexibility that is available in a tablet computer, it seems a waste to restrict it to a single user. One way to overcome this is simply to let different people use the tablet whenever they have access to it. However, since everyone likes their own music, books and movies, and different people use different types of apps, it makes much more sense to allow people to set up their individual user accounts. This creates their own personal area that can be protected from anyone else accessing it.

With tablets running Android 7.0 Nougat (and several earlier versions of Android) it is possible to add multiple users to the tablet. This means that they have their own private space on the tablet where they can access their own content and apply the settings that they want. Each separate account can also be protected by its own password. Once accounts have been set up, they can be accessed from the buttons at the top right-hand corner of the Notifications screen. Tap on a current user to view the other options.

Without user accounts, the tablet will automatically display the default account. However, if different user accounts have been set up on the tablet, a list of these accounts will be displayed in the Notifications area.

The relevant user can then tap on their own account to access it. At this point they can enter their password (or swipe the lock button) to gain access to their own account.

Customization

Once individual accounts have been set up, it is possible for each individual user to customize their account, i.e. to set the way in which their account appears and operates. This means that each user can apply their own settings, such as the appearance of the Home screen:

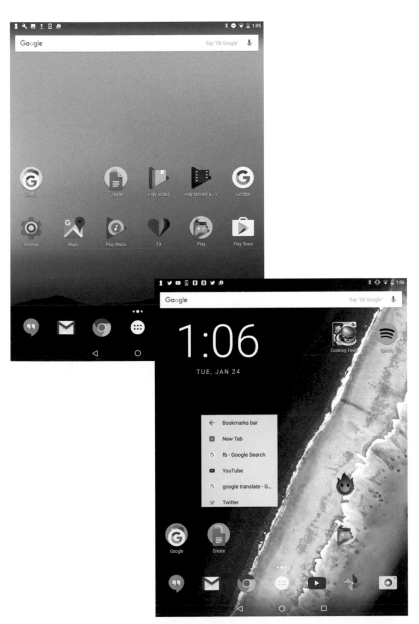

Beware

When other users are logged in to their own account you will not be able to control what they are using or looking at in terms of apps and content, unless it is a restricted profile – see page 176.

Adding Family Members

The person who first sets up the tablet is the owner of it, and they have ultimate control in terms of adding and deleting other users. To add a new user:

1 Tap on the **All Apps** button

2 Tap on the **Settings** app

3 Under the **Device** section, tap on the **Users** button

4 Tap on the **Add user** button

New users have to create a Google Account in order to use and authenticate their own account on the tablet.

172

5 Tap on the **OK** button to add the new user

Add new user?

When you add a new user, that person needs to set up their space.

Any user can update apps for all other users.

CANCEL   OK

6 Tap on the **Continue** button in the **Set up new user** window

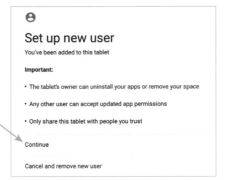

7 The new user has to enter their details, preferably with a Google Account. Tap on the **Next** button

8 Complete the setup wizard and tap on the **All Set** button to complete the new user's account

9 The **Welcome** screen notifies you that you have been added as a new user on the tablet. Tap on the **Got It** button to start using the tablet

Hot tip

Tap on the **More options** button in Step 7 and tap on the **Create account** button to create a new Google Account (if the new user does not already have one).

173

Hot tip

Each individual user can set a password that has to be entered to unlock the tablet for access to their own content. For more details about this, see pages 46-47.

Switching Between Users

It is possible to switch between users from either the Lock Screen or the Quick Settings.

From the Lock Screen

Hot tip

New users can also be added from Step 2. To do this, tap on the **Add user** button.

1 From the Lock Screen, tap on the icon for the current user at the top of the screen

2 Tap on another user's icon

3 The new user's icon is displayed at the top of the Lock Screen

From the Quick Settings

Don't forget

The most secure way to lock your tablet is with a password, using uppercase and lowercase letters, numbers and symbols.

1 Swipe down from the top of the screen to access the Quick Settings. Tap on a user's icon and then tap on it again to view other users. Tap on one to make that the active account

Guest Users

As well as being able to add new users to your tablet, you can also add guest users (with Android 5.0 and above). This can be useful for someone who wants to use your tablet on a single occasion, without the need for a permanent account. To set up a guest user:

1 From the Lock Screen, tap on the current user and tap on the **Add guest** button, or do the same from the Quick Settings by dragging down from the top of the screen

2 The **Guest** icon is displayed on the guest's Lock Screen and can also be accessed from the Quick Settings section

3 Tap on the Guest button and tap on the **Remove guest** button to delete the current guest account. Subsequent guest accounts can be set up after another guest account has been removed

Beware

If you let a guest user have access to your tablet, make sure that you lock your own account with a PIN or a password.

Restricted Profiles

Tablets are great devices for children and grandchildren; their portability and range of apps can make them the ideal device for playing games, watching videos and communicating with friends. However, these same benefits can also be a disadvantage as far as parents and grandparents are concerned – you may not always be able to see what your children are doing on the tablet, as they may be in a different place from you. One option for this is to set up a new user with a restricted profile where you can specify which apps they are able to use. To do this:

Don't forget

A range of parental control apps can also be downloaded from the Play Store, which can be used to restrict access to content, or allow access to specific apps. Some to look at include: Kids Place, Funamo, Net Nanny and Norton Family.

1 Follow the process for adding a new user as shown on page 172. Instead of adding a standard user, tap on the **Restricted profile** button

> **Add**
>
> User
> Users have their own apps and content
>
> Restricted profile
> You can restrict access to apps and content from your account

2 Tap on the **Set Lock** button and set a method for locking the screen, which is required for a restricted profile account

> Before you can create a restricted profile, you'll need to set up a screen lock to protect your apps and personal data.
>
> CANCEL   SET LOCK

3 Drag the buttons **On** for the items you want included for the user

4 Only the selected apps are available to the user with the restricted profile

11 Accessibility and Security

This chapter looks at security and accessibility issues, and finding a lost tablet.

178 Accessibility

180 Security Issues

181 About Antivirus Apps

182 Using Antivirus Apps

184 Locating Your Tablet

Accessibility

It is important for tablets to be accessible to as wide a range of users as possible, including those with visual or physical and motor issues. In Android this is done through the **Accessibility** settings. To use these:

1 Tap on the **Settings** app

Settings

2 Under the **System** section, tap on the **Accessibility** button

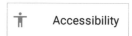

Accessibility

3 Tap on an item to turn it On or Off, or check on these items to enable functionality for increasing the text size, auto-rotating the screen and having passwords spoken as they are entered

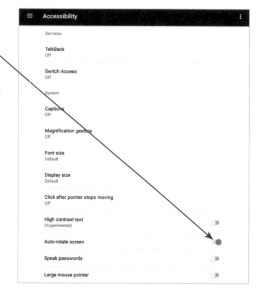

If you check On the **Large text** option, this will increase the text size for the system text on your tablet, but not necessarily the text in your apps, unless they have this functionality.

4 Tap on the **TalkBack** button in Step 3 and drag this button to **On** to activate TalkBack, whereby the tablet will provide spoken information about items on screen and those which are being accessed

5 TalkBack also provides an **Explore by Touch** function that enhances TalkBack by providing an audio description of what is on the

screen. Tap on the **OK** button to activate TalkBack

6 The active items are highlighted by a green box. Tap on an item to hear an audio description. Double-tap to activate a feature by touch

7 Tap on **Magnification gesture** in Step 3 to access the setting for zooming in on the screen by triple-tapping on it

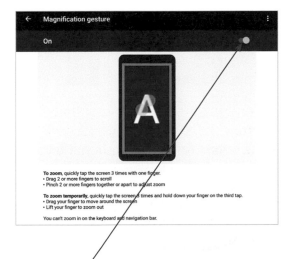

8 Drag this button On and triple-tap on the screen to zoom in on what is being viewed

Tap on the **Touch & hold delay** button in Step 3 to select the time delay for an action to take effect when you press and hold on the screen or an icon.

179

Security Issues

Security is a significant issue for all forms of computing, and this is no different for Android tablet users. Three of the main areas of concern are:

- **Getting viruses from apps**. Android apps can contain viruses like any other computer programs, but there are antivirus apps that can be used to try to detect viruses. Unlike programs on computers or laptops with file management systems, apps on a tablet tend to be more self-contained and do not interact with the rest of the system. This means that if they do contain viruses it is less likely that they will infect the whole tablet.

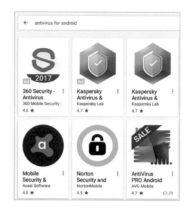

- **Losing your tablet or having it stolen**. If your tablet is lost or stolen you will want to try to get it back and also lock it remotely so that no-one else can gain access to your data and content. A lot of antivirus apps also contain a security function for lost or stolen devices.

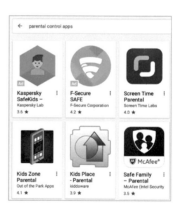

- **Restricting access for children**. If you have young children or grandchildren who are using your tablet you will want to know what they are using it for. This is particularly important for the web, social media sites, video sharing sites and messaging sites where there is the potential to interact with other people. Restricted profiles can be used for children using your tablet (see page 176) and there is also a range of parental control apps that can be downloaded from the Play Store.

About Antivirus Apps

Android tablets are certainly not immune from viruses and malware, and the FBI's Internet Crime Complaint Center (IC3) has even published advice and information about malicious software aimed at Android users. Some general precautions that can be taken to protect your tablet are:

- Use an antivirus app on your tablet. There are several of these and they can scan your tablet for any existing viruses and also check new apps and email attachments for potential problems.

- Apps that are provided in the Play Store are checked for viruses before they are published, but if you are in any doubt about an app, check it online before you download it. If you do an online search for the app, any issues related to it should be available.

- If you have a 3G or 4G connection, turn it off when you are not using it. (This will ensure that the tablet cannot make any type of cellular/mobile connection.)

- Do not download any email attachments if you are not sure of their authenticity. If you do not know the person who has sent the email then delete it.

Functionality of antivirus apps

There are several antivirus apps available in the Play Store. Search for **android antivirus apps** (or similar) to view the apps. Most security apps have a similar range of features:

- **Scanning** for viruses and malicious software (malware).

- **Online protection** against malicious software on websites.

- **Anti-theft protection.** This can be used to lock your tablet, locate it through location services, wipe its contents if they are particularly sensitive, and instruct it to let out an alert sound.

For some of the functions of antivirus and security apps a sign-in is required, such as for the anti-theft options.

A lot of antivirus and security apps are free, but there is usually a Pro or Premium version that has to be paid for.

Some antivirus apps also have an option for backing up items such as your contacts, which can then be restored to your tablet or another device if they are deleted or corrupted at all.

Using Antivirus Apps

Antivirus apps operate by scanning your tablet for malicious software. There are also usually options for displaying an activity log and additional tasks that are available.

Hot tip

It is worth downloading several of the free versions of antivirus apps, to see how you like them and to try the different functions that they have. You can use more than one antivirus app if you do not find all of the features you want in one app.

Don't forget

If any malicious software is found during a scan you will be given options for what you want to do with it, such as deleting it or quarantining it.

1 Open your antivirus app and tap on the **Scan** button to perform a new scan

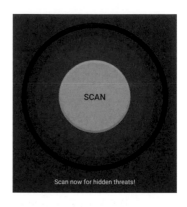

SCAN

Scan now for hidden threats!

2 A countdown box shows the progress of the scan. This is where any results and actions are displayed

17%

No threats found so far..
Apps: Ok Google enrollment

3 Tap in the **Auto-Scan Frequency** box in the **Protection** section to specify a time period for when scans are performed automatically

PROTECTION

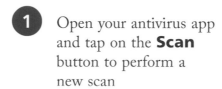

Auto-Scan Frequency
Once a week

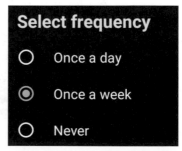

Select frequency

○ Once a day

◉ Once a week

○ Never

4 Tap on the app's menu (usually in the top right-hand corner) and tap on the **Activity Log** button, if there is one, to view tasks the app has performed

If you have a free version of an antivirus app you will not have the full range of functionality, such as web protection and backup. However, the free versions should all perform a basic scan of your tablet.

5 If there is a **Performance** option, tap on this to see the available items, including a **Task Killer**, that can be used to close down any unresponsive apps that are running

6 If there is a **Protection** option, tap on this to view additional scan options such as a **File Scanner** and **Protection settings**

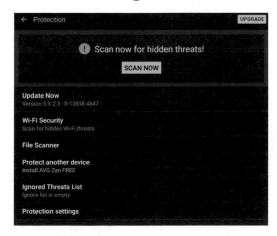

The **Protection** and **Performance** options on this page are available in the **AVG AntiVirus** app; the **Activity Log** is from the **Norton Mobile Security** app.

Locating Your Tablet

The anti-theft function of antivirus and security apps can be used to locate your tablet if it is lost or stolen. This requires three elements to be in place:

- Location-based services has to be turned on, so that the anti-theft function can use this to locate it.

- You have to sign in to the app for the anti-theft functionality. This requires a username (usually your Google Account email address) and a password. These details are used to log in to the associated website (see next page).

- You need to have access to the website associated with the app. This is where you will locate your tablet and perform any other tasks as required.

To use the anti-theft function (this example is from the AVG AntiVirus app):

Don't forget

Some anti-theft apps have a test function whereby you can hear the sound alert that will be sent to your tablet if it is lost.

1 Open your antivirus app and tap on the **Anti-Theft** button

2 You will have to register with your Google Account details. Enter these or tap on the **Create Account** button

3 You will be sent an email with instructions on using the website for finding the location of your registered tablet

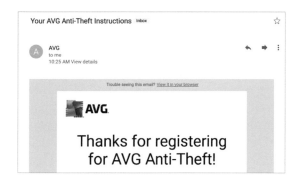

4 Click on the link in the email to go to the website

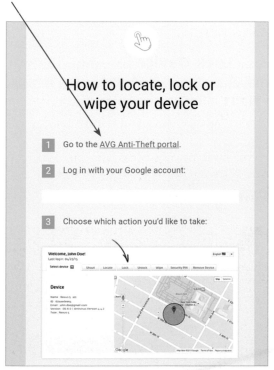

Most anti-theft apps have an option for wiping the data from a lost or stolen device. Only do this if you are worried about someone getting access to the content on your tablet, and if you know it has been backed up.

5 Log in to the website with your Google Account details

...cont'd

6 Click on the **Locate** button. The website displays a map with your tablet's location. Click on the **Lock** tab to remotely lock your tablet

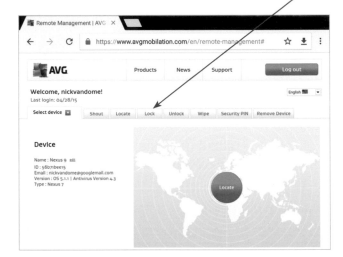

Don't forget

Click on the **Wipe** tab in Step 6 to remotely delete the content on your tablet, if you are worried about it falling into the wrong hands.

7 Enter a **Lock Device** password. This will be used to unlock your tablet when you get it back. Tap on the **Next** button to complete the process

Index

Symbols

3D graphics	15
3G/4G	
Connectivity	10, 15, 20

A

Accented letters.	
See Keyboard: Accented letters	
Accessibility	178-179
Explore by Touch	179
Magnification gesture	179
Accessories	28
Address book	69, 142-143.
See also Contacts app	
All Apps button	30
Android	9
Apps	
Interaction	19
Characteristics	12
Checking version	13
Overview	12
Updating	13
Version names	13
Android Pay	43
Anti-theft apps	181
Antivirus apps	181
Using	182-183
Apple	9
Apps	9
About	68
Adding to the Home screen	32
Built-in	69-71
Deleting	80
Downloading	78-79
Finding	76-77
Force stopping	82
Information	82
In the Play Store	74-75
Moving	33
New	74
Updating	81
Using	18-19, 68
Asus	21
Auto-correction	64
AVG AntiVirus	183

B

Back button	31
Background	
Changing	36
Battery	
Charging pack	28
Consumption	
Saving	14
Bluetooth	
Sharing photos	132
Bluetooth keyboard	28
Books	
Obtaining	114-115
Buttons	
Navigation	31

C

Calendar app	144-145
Adding events	145
Camera	26, 122
For video calls	122
Caps Lock	58
Checkbox	41
Chrome browser	149
Cleaning cloths	28
Cloud	
Saving items in	84
Connecting to the internet	
With Wi-Fi	27

Connectivity	10
Contacts app	22
Adding contacts	142
As an address book	142-143
Editing contacts	143
Cookies	156
Cover	28

D

Dictionaries	
Creating	66
Docking station	28
Doze battery saver	42

E

Ebooks	
Adding notes	118-119
Around	116-117
Bookmarks	120
Definitions	121
Deleting	116
Reading controls	116
Selecting text	118
Table of contents	116
Translations	121
Email 134.	*See also* Gmail
Adding accounts	135-136
Attachment security	181
Manual setup	135
Notifications	139
Sending	138
Settings	139
Signature	139
Using	137
Viewing	137
Entertainment apps	88-89
Events in a calendar	145

F

Facebook	140
Family history apps	98
Favorites	34
Favorites Tray	30, 34
FBI Internet Crime Complaint Center	181
File Manager	86
Finding items	48-49
Folders	
Adding to the Favorites Tray	37
Creating	37
Funamo	176

G

Games	89
Gift cards	
Redeeming	75
Gmail	134
Adding accounts	135-136
For numerous accounts	135
Google	13, 22, 48
Ok Google	51
Search options	48-51
Google+	140
Google Account	
About	22
From the Settings app	23
Obtaining	24
Payment	22
Using	146
Google Feeds	
About	52
Accessing	53
Cards	52
Customizing	55
Gmail cards	53
When traveling	159
Google Maps	70
Google Nexus	13, 20
Google Now.	*See* Google Feeds
Google Play	

Music	101
Music Manager	101
Using	100
Google Search box	30, 48, 54
Guest users	175

H

HDMI cable	
For connecting to a TV	26, 113
Headphone jack	26
Headphones	105
Health and fitness apps	94-97
Home button	31
Home screen	30
Moving between	31
Viewing	30
Hybrids	11

I

IC3. *See* FBI Internet Crime Complaint Center	
Instagram	141
iOS	9
iPad	9

J

Jelly Bean	13

K

Keyboard	
About	58-59
Accented letters	63
Advanced settings	61
Around	58-59

Auto-correction	61
Downloading additional	58
Dual functions	62
Hiding	59
Next-word suggestions	61
Settings	60-61
Shortcuts	62-63
Show correction suggestions	61
Spacebar shortcut	63
Spell checker	60
Viewing	58
Kids Place	176
KitKat	13

L

Landscape mode	40
Lenovo	21
Lifestyle apps	90-93
Linux	12
Locating your tablet	184-185
Location	43
Location-based services	
For locating your tablet	184-185
Locking	
Password	47
Pattern	47
PIN	47
Swipe	46
Your tablet	46-47
Lollipop	13
Long press	72
Losing your tablet	180

M

macOS	12
Malware	181
Managing apps	19
Marshmallow	13
Memory management	19

Microsoft   9
Micro USB port   26
Mobile data networks
    Using 3G and 4G   20
Mobile Wi-Fi unit   28
Movies   110-113
Movies and TV shows
    Renting   112
Multiple users
    Customization   171
    Overview   170-171
Multitasking with apps   72
Multi-windows   72
Music
    Add to queue   107
    Artwork   103
    Clear queue   107
    Downloading from Play Store   102-103
    Managing   107
    On Android   101
    Pinning   108-109
    Playing   104-107
        Controls   106
    Sample content   102

N

Navigation   31
Navigation buttons   30
Near Field Communication   42
Net Nanny   176
Nexus.   *See* Google Nexus
Norton Family   176
Norton Mobile Security   183
Notifications   38
    Clearing   38
    Grouped   39
    Quick Settings   39
    Replying to   39
    Settings   38
    Viewing full details   38
Notifications area   38
Notifications bar   30, 38
Nougat   13

O

Office suite apps   86
Ok Google
    For voice search   51
    Training to recognize voices   51
Online protection   181
On/Off button   26
    For sleeping a tablet   26
Organization apps   84-85
Organizing apps   37

P

Parental control apps   176
Payment
    Through a Google Account   22
Photos
    Adding   124-125
    Cropping   131
    Editing   130-131
    From email   125
    Obtaining   124
    Sharing   132
    Transferring   125
    Viewing   126-128
Photos app   122, 124-132
    Adding folders   129
    For editing photos   130-131
    For viewing photos   126-128
Pinterest   141
Pixel C   20
Play Books   22, 114
Play Movies & TV   22, 110-113
Play Music
    Subscription service   101
Play Music app
    Downloading music   102-103
    Managing music   107
    Pinning music   108-109
    Playing Music   104-106
Play Newsstand   22

Play Store   18, 22, 32
    Categories   77
    Downloading apps   78-79
    Finding apps   76-77
    Gift cards   75
    Navigating around   74-75
Portrait mode   40
Printer drivers   87
Printing   87
Productivity apps   86-87
Public wireless hotspot   15

Q

Quick Settings   30, 44
    Editing   45
Quick Switch   73
QWERTY keyboard   59
    Adding numbers from   63

R

Radio button   41
Recent Items button   31
Restricted profiles   176
Restricting access
    For children   176, 180
Rotating the screen   40
Routers for Wi-Fi access   27

S

Samsung tablets   21
Screen lock   46-47
Screen protector   28
Screen rotation   40
    Locking   40
Searching   48-50
    Voice search   49-50

Security issues   180
Settings   41-43
    Accessing   41
    Accounts   43
    Personal   43
    System   43
    Wireless & Network   42
Setting up   27
    Apps & data   27
    Google Account   27
    Google Feeds   27
    Google services   27
    Language   27
    Wi-Fi   27
SIM card   26
Skype   164-165
Sleep mode   26
Smartphones   12
Snapchat   141
Social networking   140-141
Sony Xperia   21
Spell checker   60, 64
Streaming   104
Stylus pen   28
Surface tablet   9
Swipe
    To unlock   46
Swiping
    On a web page   149

T

Tablets
    About   8-9
    Android operating system   9
    Charging   14
    Models   20-21
Tablet terms
    Apps   15
    Camera   15
    Central Processing Unit (CPU) 14
    Connectivity   15
    Graphics card   15

Memory	14
Operating System	15
Ports	15
Processor	14
Random-access memory (RAM)	14
Sensors	15
Storage	14
Touchscreen	15
Wireless	15
TalkBack	178-179
Task killer	183
Text	
Adding	64
Copy and paste	65
Selecting	65
Text size	178
Touchscreen	10
Using	16-17
Traveling	
Hotels	162
TripAdvisor	162
Tumblr	141
Turning on	26-27
TV shows	110-113
Twitter	140-141

U

UNESCO	168
USB adapter	28
USB port	26
Users	
Switching between	174

V

Videos	
Personal	
Adding	124
Viruses	180
Volume button	26

W

Wake up	
From sleep	26
Wallpaper	36
Wallpaper apps	
Downloading	36
Web browsers	
Android	148
Web pages	
Navigating around	149
Websites	
Bookmarking pages	150-151
Browser settings	155-156
Images	152
Incognito browsing	154
Links	152
Mobile versions	148
Opening pages	149
Private browsing	154
Tabs	153
Welcome screen	173
Widgets	
Adding	35
Windows	9
Wiping data	185
World Heritage sites	168

Y

YouTube	112, 141

Z

Zooming in and out	
On web pages	149